Thanks Be To God

Thanks Be To God

Robert N. Rodenmayer

Harper & Brothers New York

THANKS BE TO GOD
Copyright © 1960 by Robert N. Rodenmayer

Printed in the United States of America

FIRST EDITION
M–I
Library of Congress catalog card number: 59–5223

Dedication

To all of those, remembered
and forgotten, from whom I
have learned the goodness of
God and for whom I am thankful

Contents

7

Contents

Preface

Thanksgiving is at the heart of the Christian faith. From the earliest times a prayer of thanksgiving is the form in which the Church—the body of the faithful—expresses its relationship to God.

> *Lift up your hearts.*
> *We lift them up unto the Lord.*
>
> *Let us give thanks unto our Lord God.*
> *It is meet and right so to do.*

"A General Thanksgiving," as found in *The Book of Common Prayer*, takes some of its phrasing from a private prayer of Queen Elizabeth issued in 1596. Bishop Reynolds of Norwich (1661–76) composed it in its present form. It is said aloud by clergy and people as a communal act of gratitude "for all the blessings of this life," but especially for "the means of grace and the hope of glory."

It is hoped that this little book may be a help to some in finding the path to the meaning of thanksgiving.

ROBERT N. RODENMAYER

Berkeley, California
September, 1959

A General Thanksgiving

Almighty God, Father of all mercies, we, thine unworthy servants, do give thee most humble and hearty thanks for all thy goodness and loving-kindness to us, and to all men; We bless thee for our creation, preservation, and all the blessings of this life; but above all, for thine inestimable love in the redemption of the world by our Lord Jesus Christ; for the means of grace, and for the hope of glory. And, we beseech thee, give us that due sense of all thy mercies, that our hearts may be unfeignedly thankful; and that we show forth thy praise, not only with our lips, but in our lives, by giving up our selves to thy service, and by walking before thee in holiness and righteousness all our days; through Jesus Christ our Lord, to whom, with thee and the Holy Ghost, be all honour and glory, world without end. AMEN.

I

Almighty God, Father of all mercies . . .

It is not surprising that a god should be mighty, or that God should be Almighty. But it is surprising that God should express His Almightiness in being merciful. This is the root of our thanksgiving. We need mercy more than we need anything. Most of us begin by wanting our "rights," then we want our credit. Finally, in our blindness, we demand our "just deserts," as if we could stand it if we were to get them. I once read a fanciful English story about four men who were sitting comfortably in their club, speculating about the future. Each man in turn spoke about his hopes, his plans, his fears, and about the uncertainty of life. After a while one man said, "I would give a thousand pounds to know exactly what I will be doing a year from tonight." They all agreed. No

sooner had the words been said than the butler appeared
—a rather unusual butler—and described in detail to each
man his exact circumstances as of a year from that moment.
From then on none of them knew any peace, wondering
if the prediction were true and, if so, how it was to come
about.

This would be a difficult sort of knowledge to have.
But even worse would be a delicate awareness of the
destructive consequences of one's past actions: the far-
reaching results of the bitter word, the cruel silence, the
easy lies, the missed opportunities, the selfish invasion of
other lives. No one could stand this knowledge. It is a
mercy of God that we are not able to have it. But our
need to be forgiven is as deep as this. Our best knowledge is
to know that we are held, sustained and loved not because
of our record, but in spite of it. This is the way in which
God has revealed Himself. Our unlikeness to God has
been variously described: fallen, broken, corrupt, sinful.
His unlikeness to us—His "otherness"—is His wholeness,
His holiness.

All through the Bible this essential difference has been
perceived by prophets and poets. The author of Psalm
130 says:

> *If thou, Lord, will be extreme to mark what is done amiss,*
> *O Lord, who may abide it?*
> *For (but) there is mercy with thee;*
> *Therefore shalt thou be feared.*

Words vary in the translation of this passage but the
sense is the same. The poet who composed these lines in
his own tongue had an insight into the fact that if God,
who knows all things, were to deal with us in terms of
our actual sins—known and unknown, remembered and

forgotten—no man could stand up under it. The same poet perceives that God deals with us according to His own nature—in mercy—and, therefore, is to be held in reverence.

Jacob, son of Isaac, has a similar personal revelation, recorded in Genesis 27 and 28. A clever and wily young man, Jacob had tricked his slower-witted brother, Esau, out of his birthright. Later on, assisted, by his mother, Rebekah, he tricked him again, this time out of his dying father's blessing. Esau was ready to kill his brother for this and probably would have done so had not Rebekah urged Jacob to flee to his uncle, Laban, in Haran until Esau's anger should burn itself out. We see Jacob starting out alone into the desert. It is large, lonely and quiet. There is no one to appreciate his cleverness, no Rebekah to help him; he is on his own. When night falls he makes a solitary camp and it is there that he has in a dream a vision of God's majesty and hears God speak to him of his destiny. Waking from his dream he understands for the first time the distance between God and himself, and God's mercy in coming near. "And Jacob awaked out of his sleep, and he said, Surely the Lord is in this place; and I knew it not. And he was afraid, and said, How dreadful is this place! this is none other but the house of God, and this is the gate of heaven" (Gen. 28: 16–17).

The prophet Isaiah describes how he came to the same realization. He tells us that he was in the temple of God —no strange place to him—when he had a vision of the glory of the Lord, "high and lifted up, and his train filled the temple" (Isa. 6:1). These symbols are those of awe and majesty and wonder. Isaiah, suddenly seeing himself as a part of the picture and realizing that he does not belong in it, says, "Woe is me! for I am undone; because I am a man of unclean lips, and I dwell in the midst of a people of unclean lips; for mine eyes have seen the King, the Lord of hosts" (Isa. 6:5). But in the mercy of God the prophet is cleansed and given a job to do.

Two incidents from the New Testament will help to round out the picture. The first is in the Gospel according to St. Luke (5:1–11). Jesus has borrowed Simon Peter's fishing boat so he can talk to a crowd of people on the shore. After this he says to Peter, "Launch out into the deep, and let down your nets for a draught." Peter explains that he and his companions have been fishing all night without success, but they make another cast anyway and catch so many fish that their net breaks. Even so, they fill two small boats to the point of sinking them. Then Peter realizes for the first time who this Person is. "When Simon Peter saw it, he fell down at Jesus' knees, saying, Depart from me; for I am a sinful man, O Lord." But the Lord smiles at Peter and says, "Fear not; from henceforth thou shalt catch men."

In the Fourth Gospel (John 8:3–11) the scribes and Pharisees bring to Jesus a woman accused of adultery. They remind him that according to Jewish law she must be stoned, then ask him what *he* thinks about it. Quite obviously their only interest is more in posing a sticky question than in the woman. For some time he said nothing, then said, "He that is without sin among you, let him first cast a stone at her." * The group of accusers, looking within themselves, slowly go away one by one until the woman is left alone with Jesus. Uncondemned she stands in the presence of the Judge who is the Mercy. "Go," he says to her, "and sin no more."

Before there was a "doctrine" of God, there was God:

---

* Some ancient authorities put this passage at the end of John, some after Luke 21:38. It is a part of the gospel tradition in any case. One of the variant readings says, "He wrote on the ground the sins of every one of them."

Creator, Redeemer, Inspirer, the Judge, the Everlasting Mercy, the Holy One. This was the insight of the Hebrew people whom God chose to bear His name before the nations. God is One; He is completely who He is. Holy is whole. When we are asked to write a letter of recommendation for a friend, we strike a balance of all things we know about this person—good and bad, strong and weak —and say what we have to say. Each of us is a cluster of qualities, tensions, defenses and offerings, and all of us are changing all the time, at various speeds and at different levels. God is the only Person of whom this is not true. God is Himself, giving selfhood to all of His children; infinitely various, He is Himself without change. All of the attributes of God are the same thing. His love, His power, His judgment, His mercy, His wrath, His knowledge, His compassion are all the same as His wholeness, His holiness. God's attitude toward His created world is one of complete and unconditional good will. This is what the love of God means. This is hard for us to grasp because our own love is always conditional. We like to know that our gift is going to be accepted before we offer it. Our good will, however noble, is conditioned by our self-seeking, however subtle. We like to be thanked; in a sense we need it. God's love is poured out, broadcast as in the Parable of the Sower, on all sorts and conditions of men. But the response, whether good or bad, is not the reason for the pouring out. The only reason for that is the nature of God Himself. That is what the God of the Bible is like. Let us consider God's almightiness, His fatherhood, His mercy.

Lord Acton's remark that power tends to corrupt and that absolute power corrupts absolutely invokes agreement simply by being stated. Each of us supplies his own argument. It is easy to see how a dictator, drunk with power, adds one destructive act to another. But it is equally true in smaller ways on a smaller stage. Consider the amount of damage you could do by sitting down tonight and writing twelve anonymous letters containing the most damaging information you could think up, whether true or not. Or if your mind rejects this (and I hope it does!) think for a minute of the damage you *have* done. Power is frightening. Even in the natural world, where power is not coupled with ill will, its force awes us. The thrusting shoot of a tender plant can split a huge rock. Standing at the edge of a waterfall we hear the roar of power as we feel the earth under our feet tremble with it. No one who has been caught in a hurricane is likely to forget it. And in our times we have begun to discover the almost unbelievable reaches of nuclear energy, for good or evil.

All power is of God who is the author of the universe and the grounds of being. Only in God's hands is the use of power benign, creative, a showing forth of His love. This means that God's power is limited only by His own nature. In our case power is conditioned by responsibility. A human father has power over his child but will exercise it benevolently insofar as he accepts his responsibility to teach, nurture, protect and guide this person who is both a part of him and apart from him. But the ability to respond is itself a gift of God. Love is always a response to being loved. Our feeble and conditional good will toward any person is a reflection of God's unconditional good will toward us. Many think that the ideal form of government is benevolent despotism. This may be true but the question always arises, what is the assurance that the benevolent despot will stay benevolent? The misuse of power is probably the most difficult temptation to refuse. Only in God is it not only safe but creative, "the peacefulness of perfect power."

The disciples who came to Jesus and said, "Lord, teach us to pray," were men of faith. They were pious Jews who had been praying all their lives. The reason for their request was, I think, not the absence of the practice of prayer but their observation of a relationship with God unknown to them. Jesus said, "When you pray, say Our Father." This was the secret of the relationship. The same God who made the whirling universe and everything in it shows forth his power in fatherhood. A poet of the Old Testament has an insight into this truth when he says, "Like as a father pitieth his own children, even so is the Lord merciful unto them that fear him" (Ps. 103:13). Jesus makes it explicit in his own human relationship with God the father. The Power at the heart of the universe partakes of personality. God reveals Himself in a family relationship. This is our hope, not only of salvation but of brotherhood.

The judgment of God is an expression of His fatherhood, His love. It means that God deals in a real way with a real situation. When we use the word "judgment" in common speech we imply the same thing. A person asked to be judge at a debate, for instance, is expected to decide as objectively as he can which team made the better argument, regardless of his opinion of any of the debaters when they are not debating. In short, as judge, he is expected to tell the truth. When we say that a person has good judgment in operating an automobile we mean that he deals fairly with the real data: the condition of the car, the condition of the driver, the condition of the road, the weather, the time of day. In short he tells, or acts out, the truth. This is true of the judgment of God on individuals and in history. God cannot be cajoled, lobbied or "influenced," as all of us try to deal with each other. He is "Almighty God unto whom all hearts are open, all desires known, and from whom no secrets are hid." Fundamental to this He is the Father who cares infinitely about the well-being of His children. This is the reason for His judgment.

Suppose that you have a child, say eight or nine years old, and that you live on a busy street. You have explained to your child that he is not to cross the street unless some grown-up person is with him. People would not want to run him down but they might not see him in time to avoid it. All of this is understood, accepted and agreed to. Now suppose that as you come home the next day you see your child dodging across the street narrowly missing being struck by a car. You have, it seems to me, three live options. You can pretend that you did not see the incident, which would be dealing dishonestly. You can say to your child, "Remember what I told you yesterday about not crossing the street? Well, don't give it a thought, I didn't mean a word of it." This would leave the child in a formless universe where right and wrong have no meaning. It is like saying to a person that nothing is expected of him, nothing matters, "nobody would blame you." This is not only dishonest, it is destructive.

The only alternative left is to enter into judgment with the child. His responsibility was understood and accepted and violated. Many opinions might be given as to what the nature of this judgment should be, but the reason for it will be the same as the reason for the original ban on street crossing: because the parent cares about the child. If there were no love here the parent would have no inner reason to concern himself whether the child were run over or not.

This is, of course, a part of the biblical idea of covenant. God enters into a relationship—makes a covenant—with His people. The promises are variously expressed to the patriarchs of the Hebrew nation, but involved in all of them is the concept of God's loving concern, His care, His choosing; the Almighty Father alive and active in the events of history, in particular, in the life of His chosen people. The people's part of this covenant is allegiance to God ("the fear of the Lord") and, therefore, a moral responsibility. Righteous demands are made upon them and, as in the case of the child on the busy street, when these demands, understood and accepted, are violated God must enter into judgment with His people because He cares about them. Love can never turn into nothingness.

When the prophet Amos says to the faithless court of Jeroboam II, in the name of the Lord, "You only have I known of all the families of the earth: therefore I will punish you for all your iniquities" (Amos 3:2), he is saying that God must enter into judgment with His people because of His love for them. The insight of the prophet Hosea is that God deals compassionately with His people even when they have proved unfaithful to Him; He takes them back, He gives them a second chance. It was left for the nameless prophet called the Second Isaiah (Chapters 40–55), probably the summit of Old Testament faith, to perceive that God Himself enters into the sufferings of His people. "But he was wounded for our transgressions, he was bruised for our iniquities: the chastisement of our peace was upon him; and with his stripes we are healed" (Isa. 53:5).

There is good news in God's judgment because it is creative. When we are judged innocent in a court of law we are right where we were before the action started. When we are judged by Almighty God, father of all mercies, as we are every day, we are held in a living and loving relationship. The truth is told about us but it is a saving truth, a truth in the light of which a man may turn and live again.

There is a paradox in judgment; we fear it and at the same time we crave it. We are reluctant to have our position defined, especially when this involves a negative judgment, but there is something in it satisfying to us at the same time. We know where we are. There is a piece of good news in being brought to the end of the road. A man who has dodged the police successfully for years will sometimes feel compelled to give himself up, perhaps in a distant city, just to live in the same moral universe as the unknowns with whom he walks the streets. There is a necessity to face the music, a security to be found in playing out the game in its own terms. This is to say that the truth is ultimately satisfying. And the truth at the heart of the universe—the judgment of God—is the divine truth-telling coupled with the divine compassion. The clean, straight good will of God is His grace. The power is trustworthy. The judgment is saving.

Father of all mercies. The almost incredible fact that God shows forth His almightiness in being merciful is the fact at the center of the Gospel. This is God's response to our deepest and most common need, the need to be forgiven. The wisest and truest words that we can take on our lips is the prayer, "Have mercy upon us."

The word "mercy" is not much in common use. We hear it sometimes in the phrase "to throw oneself on the mercy of the court." The roots of the word appear to mean reward, to receive as a share, and this is illuminating. The mercy of God is His gift to us of participation in His own nature. We live under the mercy because God, above all else, is the giver of gifts.

II

. . . we, thine unworthy servants . . .

One of the best-known stories in the civilized world is that of the Prodigal Son (Luke 15:11–32). The young man having left home to seek his fortune, runs through his money, exhausts the interest of his fair-weather friends and gets a job feeding pigs to keep himself alive. Meditating on his broken dreams he decides to go home where he belongs, where even his father's servants are better off than he is. On his way home he practices a speech to say to his father—a speech which includes the phrase, "I am no more worthy to be called thy son; make me as one of thy hired servants."

Many have speculated about this story. Is the young man being honest? Or is this a well-rehearsed procedure to improve his condition at his father's expense? It seems to me that the point of the story is the same in either case: the nature of God who seeks and saves that which is lost. The mercy is unconditional, no matter how conditional the approach to it may be. Human motives are mixed. God's motive is one, to create and make new.

On the record of how the boy has spent his time, his resources, his freedom, there does not seem to be a lot of worthiness. No matter what he may think or how he may act, the record is not a very good one; he *is* unworthy. One of the real differences between this boy and his elder brother is that he acknowledges his unworthiness (let us suppose that he is telling only *half* of the truth), while the stay-at-home brother perceives no unworthiness in himself at all. Quite the contrary. So we have three levels of attitude in the parable. God's attitude is one of generosity and welcome, of unconditional good will. The father in the story might be fooled, though he is willing to be for the joy of having the boy home safe and sound. God, who knows the secrets of the heart, is not fooled but is more willing to take us back than we are to come to Him. And it *is* at His expense. The elder boy cannot afford to be a fool; it would be too expensive to his pride.

The fact is that at the end of the story both boys are unworthy but one of them in admitting it, however partially, is at home again and risen from the dead while the other, strong in his "worthiness," is outside because he would not go in.

The word "worthy" occurs in another familiar passage, that which tells of the soldier whose servant Jesus healed (Matt. 8:8–13). This centurion, presumably an officer in the army of Herod Antipas, entreats Jesus to heal his servant "who was dear to him" (says the Lukan version). Jesus says simply, "I will come and heal him." It is then that the officer says bluntly, "Lord, I am not worthy that thou shouldst come under my roof; but speak the word only, and my servant shall be healed." The centurion is speaking the truth; he is unworthy but, again, his acknowledgment of the truth makes it possible for him to receive the loving-kindness of God. The mercy of God is constant and is always offered, but God coerces no man. He pursues us only with His love, waiting for us to turn and receive it. This is not easy. It is always easier to give a gift than to accept one. And the gift most difficult to accept (because most demanding) is the gift of mercy, of forgiveness. It involves self-judgment and can be received only in humbleness.

There is no reason for the love of God. One cannot argue to it from any point outside itself. It is literally absurd. It is a gift and the gift which makes any other love possible. If God had good sense, as the world judges, He long ago would have found more profitable servants than any of us who try to serve Him. But the fact that God continues to love the unlovely, the unlovable, is the fact that makes it possible for us to change for the better. The unworthy servant is no less unworthy; his acceptance by God, and his acceptance of his acceptance, bestows worthiness upon him.

There is a very reasonable speech which goes something like this: "I gave you a job because I knew your father but you have been a disappointment to me from the first day. We are engaged in an important enterprise here as you must understand. I have given you a number of chances, I have been very patient, but now I am sure you will see that I have no choice but to let you go." Given the alleged facts, no one would call this statement unreasonable. Mercifully for us it is not God's speech, He never makes it. We can go to hell if we insist on it and God will permit us to do so—He gives us the dignity of doing what we insist on—but it will be our doing, not His.

God does make righteous demands upon us; it is this which gives integrity to our relationship with Him. Being made in the "image of God" means at least two things. It means that the creature is able to communicate with the Creator; we can know and love God in Christ, in and through the people of God. We can never know and love as we are known and loved. But the lines are open, prayer is more than autosuggestion, redemption takes place on an ordinary street, there can be a glory in the commonplace. The other meaning of "image of God" is that we are under judgment, God is going to tell the truth about us. It will be the truth in mercy, the truth in love, but it will be the truth. This is the basis of sanity.

The teaching about forgiveness—the principle of the Lord's Prayer—is clearly set forth in the parable of the unforgiving servant (Matt. 18:23–35). This vivid story is really a play in three acts. A king wishes to settle accounts with his servants. One is brought to him who owes him ten thousand talents (ten million dollars!) and the king demands payment. The servant pleads for patience and is forgiven the whole debt. He then goes to one of his fellow servants and demands payment of a debt which amounts to about twenty dollars. When the man pleads for patience he is refused and is put into prison until the debt should be paid. When news of this happening reaches the king he summons the servant, reminds him of the merciful way in which he was treated, and asks "Should not you have had mercy on your fellow servant, as I had mercy on you?" And at the end of the story the ungrateful servant is in debtors' prison because he did not forgive his brother from his heart.

26

A number of things may be learned here. The first is that the nature of God is to be merciful to all men. It follows that the most direct and imitative way for a man to be godly is to copy this characteristic attitude of God's in dealing with men. But it is not simply imitation; it is the gift of power to do it. It is possible for us to be forgiving when we have accepted forgiveness. This is not a slide-rule transaction as our rendering of that phrase in the Lord's Prayer seems to indicate. God's forgiveness of us is not limited or conditioned by our willingness to forgive others. Rather, it is God's forgiving us—His thawing us out, if you will—and our acceptance of that gift, which makes forgiveness on our part possible. Forgiveness precedes repentance, draws repentance out of us.

Let me illustrate. A self-righteous man who is a pillar of society locally, regular in church attendance and successful in business, has two daughters in their late teens. The younger girl, about seventeen, a warm, attractive person, becomes pregnant while unmarried. She tells her mother who tells her father, for whom the news is shattering. "What," he asks, "will people say about *my* daughter, about *me?*" Hurt, bitter and disappointed he summons a family council and invites the pastor to attend, presumably to agree with his injured feelings. He does not do so. In fact, as the discussion proceeds it becomes evident that the pastor and the girl's father represent almost opposite points of view. Finally the man, facing the pastor, explodes, "Do you mean to sit there and say I just have to *take* this?" "Yes," said the pastor, "that's where you start."

Well, as you can see, he was not up to doing that, his pride was too strong to let him. The daughter left home, protecting herself as well as she could with her own pride. It was all she had. And pride begets pride.

Now consider what might have happened, and does happen. At the family council, with or without the pastor, the father might have said something like this: "Jane, I am sorry this happened, sorry for you and for me and for all of us. But it did happen and it is partly my fault. There will be some rough spots but we will close in as a family and do our best to help. Mostly, your mother and I want you to know that you are still our daughter and we love you. Nothing can change that, no matter what happens."

If that had happened, the girl would have been *able* to come to her father's arms and to say through her tears, "O Daddy, I'm so sorry!" Forgiveness makes repentance possible. The writer of the Epistle to the Ephesians says, "Let all bitterness, and wrath, and anger, and clamour, and evil speaking, be put away from you, with all malice: and be ye kind one to another, tenderhearted, forgiving one another, even as God for Christ's sake hath forgiven you" (Eph. 4:31–32). A forgiven person has something to give away.

The pilgrimage from worthiness to unworthiness to being accounted worthy, may be seen graphically illustrated in the life of St. Paul. Saul, as he was when we first meet him, had everything to lose and nothing to gain by becoming a Christian. His worthiness was the worthiness of the world and it adds up to a rather impressive total as we learn later in his own words when he is standing trial for his life (Acts 21–23). Accused of being an Egyptian and the leader of a murderous mob he says, "I am a Jew of Tarsus, a city in Cilicia, a citizen of no mean city." Beginning his defense he says of his education, "I [was] brought up in this city [Jerusalem] at the feet of Gamaliel, and taught according to the perfect manner of the law of the fathers." Further, defining his religious position, he says, "I am a Pharisee, the son of a Pharisee."

Regarding Roman citizenship, a prized possession, we find this interesting passage. "And as they bound him with thongs, Paul said unto the centurion that stood by, Is it lawful for you to scourge a man that is a Roman, and uncondemned? When the centurion heard that, he went and told the chief captain, saying, Take heed what thou doest: for this man is a Roman. Then the chief captain came, and said unto him, Tell me, art thou a Roman? He said, Yea. And the chief captain answered, With a great sum obtained I this freedom. And Paul said, But I was free born. Then straightway they departed from him which should have examined him: and the chief captain also was afraid, after he knew that he was a Roman, and because he had bound him."

Added to the worthiness of the world, the customary securities, this man was further secured by a persecuting zeal. Familiar to all of us is his appearance in the book of Acts "breathing out threatening and slaughter" on his way to Damascus, charged with searching out and arresting "the disciples of the Lord."

But he reckoned without the Lord, as we often do. This is, I suppose, the real meaning of secularism, the supposition that we live in a one-story universe, with no demands except those we make on ourselves and on each other. And, again like ourselves, Paul was ministered to by God through the people of God. The disciples of the Lord had something to say to him, probably without knowing it, about the problems of freedom and security. Outstanding among these teachers was the young man, Stephen, falsely accused of blasphemy and in whose trial Paul was involved. The first reference to the man later to be the first apostle to the gentile world is at the stoning of Stephen. The record says simply, "They cast him out of the city and stoned him; and the witnesses laid down their garments at the feet of a young man whose name was Saul" (Acts 7:58). Years later, at the time of his trial, Paul recalls this incident which had stayed alive in his memory. He says, "And when the blood of thy martyr Stephen was shed, I also was standing by, and consenting unto his death, and kept the raiment of them that slew him" (Acts 22:20).

At the stoning of Stephen we are presented with the picture of a successful young lawyer, thinking furiously. Something has gone wrong with his securities. Then comes the road to Damascus when Paul, unable to resist any longer, is seized by the Lord and his new life begins. This is what God does with our worthiness, this is conversion. Our former values become valueless—in fact, a nuisance—in order that we may find, as disciples of the Lord, our real freedom.

Ask yourself this question, to be answered in your secret mind: What do I want most? The answer to that question is the index of your freedom. In writing to the church at Philippi, Paul uses the bluntest of terms to describe those things which he used to value most, for in Christ he has found all that he needs. Through faith in the living God, operating in the lives of men in this world, Paul has found his own insufficiency, the saving outreach of God in Christ, his own salvation through faith. He is the same man he was before: intense, sometimes vain, frequently irascible, tempted often to be the clever lawyer—the blur of words, the wall of thought—but knowing what he knew, that he had been adopted, accounted as righteous, treated as if worthy because of the saving act of Christ the Lord. This he knew and this he preached.

St. Paul describes himself as the *slave* of Christ. The

Bible uses a number of words, with different shades of meaning, all of which are translated in the Authorized Version as "servant." Strongest among them (literally "slave") is that used by St. Paul to indicate his relationship to his Risen Lord. The modern mind boggles at this word. No American or Englishman, for instance, warms to the idea of being a slave to anybody; in fact the history of Western Europe since the end of the feudal period has been a slow and often a violent progress toward political freedom for the common man. In our times one of the most important phenomena is the upsurging of millions in Asia and Africa toward the same goal. What then of Paul's "slavery" to Christ, especially when we recall that this is the same man who said with some pride, "But I was free born"?

The answer is to be found, I think, in the meaning of the words "worthy" and "unworthy." Before his conversion—his being shaken up, turned around, revolutionized, remade by the Lord—Paul was not only worthy, he was a success. To put it in contemporary terms, he was making money and had a good future. Slowly he became convinced that he could not be saved (safe) by the Law; that is, he could not find peace or security or wholeness by fulfilling, however carefully, requirements and obligations and duties. They could not feed him and left him, in fact, empty. What then? He perceived a freedom, even a joy, in the weak captives which he, Saul the strong, brought to book. It was puzzling. Then came the business of Stephen's trial and stoning; "and he kneeled down, and cried with a loud voice, Lord, lay not this sin to their charge." After that, full of crusading zeal and bolstered with the last supplies of his worthiness, Paul set out for Damascus and met the Lord. Now he was done for, washed up, annihilated. In an agony of spirit he asked and answered his own question, "Who art thou, Lord?" Years later, plagued by weariness, opposition and physical disability, he got the same answer, "My grace is sufficient for thee: for my strength is made perfect in weakness" (2 Cor. 12:9).

Archbishop William Temple once said that the sin of the world exists not because a few people are spectacularly sinful but because most of us are as good as we are, and no better. There is a solidarity of unworthiness in which we all partake. We are unworthy servants. Equally true and constant is the goodness of God who shows forth His power in being merciful. No one can earn the love of God because no one can earn the love of anybody. Love is a gift and the response to a gift. The best thing we know is that God is merciful in the face of our unworthiness, that in Christ He makes us worthy. And in the strength of that truth we can pray.

III

*. . . do give thee most humble
and hearty thanks . . .*

The heart of thanksgiving is an awareness of the nature
of the gift. The person who almost miraculously escapes
sudden death on the highway is grateful for the gift in
the first place. Otherwise he may simply consider himself
lucky. He *is* lucky, of course, if he escapes with his life;
whatever else he feels will depend on his whole attitude
toward life and living. One who has been unable to leave
his bed for weeks because of sickness or accident can appreciate the joy of walking slowly across the room and
looking out the window if he thinks that life is worth
looking at.

The Pharisee who prays out loud in the temple, "God,
I thank thee, that I am not as other men are" (Lk. 18:11),
and then goes on to make a list of other men's shortcom-

ings, is not being thankful at all except for his own smug-
ness. He is assuming his own righteousness, as well as
the sinfulness of others, and swaggering in the presence
of his Judge. It is impossible for this man to be thankful,
even supposing that everything he says is true, because
he is unaware of the nature of the gift which is God's
goodness. He is too interested in his own goodness to
see God's. On the other hand, when St. Paul says, "I thank
my God through Jesus Christ for you all, that your faith
is spoken of throughout the whole world" (Rom. 1:8),
this is genuine thanks. He is aware both of the fact of
faith and of its source.

In the incident of the ten lepers healed by Jesus (Lk.
17:11–17), only one of them returned to give thanks for
his cure. Only one was aware of the nature of the gift—the
goodness of God. One supposes that the other nine were
glad enough to be whole again but that was the end of
it.

After all, why should one be thankful? Is it not enough
that a good thing is accomplished without any necessity
for being thankful about it? Thankfulness neither in-
creases nor decreases the thing itself. This is true. If one is
saved alive from a situation in which he might well have
been killed the fact remains that he is alive and not dead.
He may be thankful for his deliverance or he may not be.
If he is thankful (and in this prayer he says that he is),
it is because he knows that he has a relationship to the
world in which he lives and to its author. He has a reason
for living, something to live *for*.

What does one live for? One can take a materialistic
view as the temper of his days and live with it as his guid-
ing principle. It has certain advantages in that things can
be seen and handled and possessed. A part of this is good
and necessary. It was Jesus himself who taught us to ask

for our daily bread. Some things are neecssary to life itself—food, clothing and shelter, in the old phrase. Added to that is the fun that we all have in acquiring a new (though perhaps only new to us) piece of furniture to live with. It may be a chair, a rug, a painting or a shelf of books or a stove. Married couples will remember the satisfaction of being able slowly to replace the orange crates with something more substantial. The key seems to be an ability to keep the things themselves in their proper scale in one's total view of importance and usefulness. It sometimes happens that married couples, no longer young, look back on their orange-crate days as the happiest they have known together, even though their present state may be luxurious in comparison. A young woman once remarked about her father, a self-made, successful, substantial and "important" businessman, "My father has everything he thought he wanted and nothing that he wants." This is the tragedy of the self-defeating inward spiral. About it Jesus said, "What shall it profit a man if he gains the whole world and loses his own soul?" It is really a question of ownership. I know a man who has made a good living over the years and who owns a great many things. He has two houses, carefully equipped with burglar alarms and special locks. He has three cars and a pick-up truck for the country place which has a full-time private watchman when the owner is not in residence. He has some costly furniture and all the latest gadgets. He also has ulcers. Actually the things own *him*.

There is a freedom in not needing much but in enjoying much without possessing it. In his *Travels with a Donkey*—one of the most charming travel books ever written—Robert Louis Stevenson tells of an incident when he is camping out alone in a pine woods at a high point in the Lozère range of Southern France. It is a beautiful piece of writing conveying the joy of living intensely, quietly and gratefully under a wide and starry sky "where God keeps an open house." Full of the change and wonder of the place as he packs up to leave in the morning, he feels moved to make an offering for the hospitality he has enjoyed. He says, "And so it pleased me, in a half-laughing way, to leave pieces of money on the turf as I went along, until I had left enough for my night's lodging." This is whimsical, no doubt, and impractical but it is at the same moment a rash and refreshing response to the lavishness of God!

The person who has decided, perhaps on quite understandable grounds, that the possession of things is the most important goal in living has, at least, a definable position. Whether he collects rents, houses, automobiles or whatever else appears to him to be desirable, he is putting up a barrier against change, against attack, against mortality. After a while the barrier gets to be an end in itself and the man who originally built it for himself shrinks in significance behind it. The trouble with living by bread alone is that it is bread alone.

Or one can live for pleasure—either the pleasure of the moment or one elaborately devised. There is something to be said for this point of view. But "eat, drink and be merry for tomorrow we die" has a note of desperation in it. One cannot always be merry when he sets out deliberately to accomplish it. But there is much to be enjoyed. A good meal with friends or family, the smell of freshly baked bread, "the kindly fruits of the earth"—these are good things. The world of the senses which God made is an infinitely variegated world into which we are invited at birth. Taste, touch, sound—or pungency, texture and cadence, for instance—are gates into a delightful land. The knowingness of sight—faces, colors, movements, lights and shadows—is never ending. God looked on it in the beginning and said that it was good.

Further, the adventure of arts and crafts is at the end of our fingers. A man sits down at a concert piano and plays with skill and grace and discipline. Beauty is born. Minds are rested. Spirits are healed. People go away knowing perhaps not more, but better than they did before. An artist puts on canvas a part of what he sees in his inward eye—he can never do more than that—and makes a window through which we see more than we ever could have seen without his help. There is clean, functional beauty in a good tool—pleasing to the eye and the hand and the spirit. There is joy in the arch of a well-made bridge and a well-designed house has a presence of its own.

Pleasure goes wrong, becomes displeasure, when it reaches in instead of out. The child in nursery school, making his first excursions into the world of color and form, realizes his pleasure when he takes his work of art home and Mother says it is fine. The man of sensitivity who sits at the piano invoking beauty in sound has something to give away, a good thing to be shared. Pleasure pursued for its own sake whether of the bodily senses or the finest of the fine arts, is the inward spiral again. It is self-defeating. It needs to be offered, to be used, even to be sacrificed. Then it becomes a way of knowing and the knowledge is good.

Some people live for power and this is the worst of the inward spiral. There is nothing more frightening than having power over other human beings. It is a knowledge that we are not supposed to have, should not have, for in our hands it is demonic. We have already thought of the destructive quality of power when linked with ill will. Here I will suggest that the invocation of power as a design for living ends in loneliness. It is suicide of the spirit, often of the body as well. The Faust legend, which occurs in many forms and in many literatures, is a true insight. A man makes a pact with the prince of darkness —for a price, himself—to gain the power of secret knowledge or the ability to control events and to make people do his bidding. The pact is fulfilled, the power enjoyed. Then comes the awful moment of payment. The man is alone, all alone, with his fate. "Ah Mephistopheles!"

> *Cut is the branch that might have grown full straight,*
> *And burnéd is Apollo's laurel bough*
> *That sometime grew within this learned man.*

Then there is the person who decides to maintain a position of disinterested detachment. He is not to be fooled as ordinary men are fooled. He knows that the possession of many things is a form of bondage. He knows that the pursuit of pleasure for its own sake is a man pursuing himself. The college sophomore making a spectacle of himself has a cerain youthful attractiveness; the same man twenty years later, loudly trying to recapture his youth at the homecoming game, is a sad sight. The man of detachment knows this.

He holds himself aloof from power, preferring to view the human comedy from the side lines. He will not become involved and so will escape being hurt. The picture has a certain appeal. It looks cool and urbane and sophisticated—like Richard Cory, "clean favored and imperially slim." This is the Man of Reason who considers life with judicious calm. He builds about him a discreet wall to keep others out of his life and, in so doing, keeps himself from the expense of sharing theirs. The trouble is, of course, that it is a pose which is supportable only as long as the emotional weather is fine. But what happens to this man when he loses his temper, or is unjustly attacked, or falls in love—all quite irrational states? The pose falters, the façade cracks.

Each of these roles has a positive and a negative element, a creative and a destructive dimension. The negative way differs only in the path that is followed: things in themselves, power, pleasure, aloofness—each for its own sake, the inward spiral. The creative way lies in the realization of a good thing to be shared; things to be enjoyed together, beauty to be given away, power to be offered, the ability to discriminate as a guide for choices. All of these spring from thanksgiving, from having received knowingly from a boundless source of goodness.

To respond gladly to the gifts one has been given and at the heart of the matter, to respond gladly to the God who is the giver of all good gifts, is to begin to taste life as it is. We tend to cheat ourselves and to settle for less than is being offered. Paganism prompts us to say sometimes, "Things are going so well that I am sure something is about to go wrong. Nothing could be this good." The thankfulness that grows from our life in God teaches us to know that it *is* this good because God is good.

The phrase "humble and hearty thanks" at first reading seems confusing, almost a confusion in terms. On second thought it is very perceptive. Humble here means fitting, in the old New England sense; appropriate. Hearty has its face value of whole, straightforward, enthusiastic; "up to the brim." I recall an incident in a large city hospital clinic, more than twenty years ago, which helps to illustrate these words for me. There was the usual large waiting room filled with patient people standing in line or sitting in folding chairs around the sides of the room, numbered slips in their hands, waiting to be called. It was a room full of numbered anonymity—unnaturally quiet people, having exchanged numbers for names, waiting hopefully to be helped.

As the line moved slowly forward each person came eventually to a table behind which a nurse sat who took down the necessary data. My position was that of a theological student in clinical training and I stood behind the nurse waiting to pick up a sheaf of records. As I stood there I observed the line. In the strangeness of the situation most of the people tried to make themselves as anonymous as possible, so I could not help noticing half way down the line a man who appeared to be completely at ease. He was dressed in ordinary working clothes and at first glance was not distinguishable from those around him. Then one noted the composure. He looked to be rather more completely who he was than most people, certainly than most people there. Whatever bodily complaint had brought him, his face had the look of well-being, of peace. Curiously and with a sort of responsive pleasure I watched his slow progress up the line. When it came his turn the nurse asked his name and address, which he gave. His age was fifty-seven.

"Last residence?"

"Damascus."

"Occupation?"

The man smiled and held out his hands, palms up. They were good hands, strong and square and capable. He said, "My father was a master stone cutter. I am a master stone cutter." That was all—not a boast but a statement of fact and a simple pride in it, a thankfulness. Humble and hearty thanks. He knew what he knew and was composed in that knowledge. In a sense it gave him a handle on the whole universe.

An act of thanksgiving, however small and unimportant

it may seem, always enlarges one's horizons. I have a friend who makes a practice of writing letters from time to time to authors or composers or painters, saying a simple and sincere "thank you" for what she has received from them. She has no expectation of meeting the people to whom she writes and she is not an autograph collector. She is, in fact, a cripple but her life is enriched and, I have no doubt, so are the lives of the persons to whom she writes her sensitive and understanding thanks.

Sometimes on an impulse a person will write a letter to one he has not seen for years, recalling an act of kindness or a word of encouragement treasured and used over the years and thereby set up a whole chain reaction of thanksgiving. Such a letter was written a year or two ago by a busy, successful and thoughtful physician to an old man about to retire from a long career as a teacher in a medical school. It was not an effusive letter but a genuine and uncalculating expression of thanks for the older man's insight which had benefited the writer and his patients for half a lifetime. A letter like that is priceless though it costs nothing and, like mercy, blesses both the giver and the receiver.

Another example. A middle-aged woman busy in her own affairs took time to call on an old lady who was bedridden, just for the sake of calling on her. She stayed for an hour or so talking about what she had been doing, bringing the brisk air of an active life into a little room. When the caller got up to leave the old lady said, "I didn't know you could be so kind." The words are both accusing and enlightening. Thanksgiving is something to be received and given away—humble and hearty. The instruction "to give thanks for all men" at first glance seems absurd and unthinkable. Those impossible people! Then as one begins to see himself with a little honesty, to notice with what generosity he is often regarded and on what slender grounds, the assignment takes on the edge of possibility. It may become an adventure, with many chances for disappointment or worse, but it leads to a rich involvement in life itself.

Thanksgiving is involvement for good. Many benefits are received for which there is no conscious feeling of thanksgiving. The benefits are none the less beneficial but a dimension in living has been missed. Consider again the ten lepers healed by Jesus, only one of whom when he saw that he was healed, returned to give thanks. All ten had asked for mercy and all ten had received it. Nine went their way, no doubt delighted at their cure, but giving no thanks to the author of it. The one who did so was no better off physically than his companions but because of his humble and hearty thanks he had a living relationship with the Lord which the others did not have.

We know from passages like this one that God accepts our thanks, our self-offering. This is a remarkable thing because it means that God accepts us into Himself. The fact that He is the author of the created world, of however many universes there may be, including the people who live in and enjoy it—this is remarkable enough. But the fact that He is personally involved in it is more so. This is the fundamental reason for our humble and hearty thanks.

There is a considerable difference between expecting thanks and accepting thanks. The person who does "nice things" in order to be thanked is not only tiresome but self-defeating. We all know this sort of person and, at times, we have all been this sort of person. It is another version of the person who always has his feelers out to be hurt, who registers the smallest current which can be interpreted as a slight. Those who need always to be thanked will very soon not be and, worse than that for them, will be avoided.

The ability to accept thanks, however, without cold-ness on the one hand or wallowing on the other, is a quality of maturity. Thanksgiving is a gift, whether in giving or receiving. Let me go back for a moment to the child who makes a work of "art" in nursery school. He is proud of it; it is a part of himself, expressed. He brings it home triumphantly or shyly, depending upon his nature, and presents it to his mother. She accepts the gift and thanks him for it; a gift is bestowed for a gift. If the child expects thanks it is because of his previous experi-ence of his mother's attitude. But the thanks is a gift in any case. She does not *have* to thank him; she might tell him, absent-mindedly or busily, to put the thing on the table, she will look at it later. But if she does respond generously and spontaneously it will be because she is thankful, because her gifts have been received with thanks-giving. And ultimately, all the way up, because her thanks-giving has been and is being received by God.

Thanksgiving is an offering of oneself and a vehicle for things which cannot be said. And if it is the best one has, whether it is a nursery school production or a life of service, it is enough. An English contemporary, Harold Sly, writes: "Jesus once wanted to feed five thou-sand people. He could not do it while He remained empty-handed. But all that anyone could give Him was five cobs and a couple of sprats. It was all they could give Him. Therefore it was enough. And if that had not been brought to Him, I suppose that the feeding of the five thousand would never have taken place."

It appears to be true that an act of thanksgiving, springing from an inner attitude of thankfulness, not only enlarges one's horizon but also makes possible an expansion of the spirit, a relatedness, a power. Since God is all the power there is, and since He shows forth that power chiefly in being merciful, our humble and hearty thanks for Him and to Him becomes an avenue of grace between creature and creator, between man who needs and God who gives.

There are three kinds of giving: grudge giving, duty giving and thanksgiving. Grudge giving says, "I have to," duty giving says, "I ought to," thanksgiving says, "I want to." The first comes from constraint, the second from a sense of obligation, the third from a full heart. Nothing much is conveyed in grudge giving since "the gift without the giver is bare." Something more happens in duty giving but there is no song in it. Thanksgiving is an open gate into the love of God.

IV

*For all thy goodness
and loving-kindness to us,
and to all men . . .*

The consideration of the nature of man and how he regards himself is as old as mankind, though these two aspects of the problem do not necessarily go hand in hand. In the last few years scores of interesting books have enlightened us on the subject of primitive man and his development. The study of anthropology (the science of man) and of archaeology (the study of history from the relics and remains of antiquities) has captured the imagination of the general reader as never before. Due to a series of systematic excavations and to the light that has been shed on ancient cultures, scholars will be kept busy for years sorting out and classifying the new knowledge that has turned up. And the investigation into the living past will go on, each explorer eager to make a find that will illuminate an area which up to that time was unknown or guessed at. New tools, new methods of research and inquiry have made the search more practical and more efficient. Scarcely a week goes by that something new is not discovered.

Along with this goes man's inquiry about himself. No one knows how far back in history this reaches—certainly long before any written records we have; it is as old as speculation itself. The Hebrew psalmist, addressing himself to God wrote:

> *When I consider the heavens, even the work of thy fingers;*
> *The moon and the stars which thou hast ordained;*
> *What is man, that thou art mindful of him?*
> *And the son of man, that thou visitest him?*
> *Thou madest him lower than the angels,*
> *To crown him with glory and worship* [*Ps. 8:3–5*].

This poet has the insight to raise the two basic questions which have always been at the heart of man's inquiry about himself. Assuming the existence of God — in fact he begins and ends his poem with a burst of praise — he wonders how God who is the creator of the universe could bother about man. And in the same breath he identifies the other basic problem, that of the two natures of man—man against himself. Much has been written in recent times about this latter question, and much that is helpful, but the question itself is one of the oldest in the world.

Our psalmist believes that God *does* care about man, is "mindful" of him; the question he raises is why He should be. I have suggested before that there is no reason why God should love us; He appears to do so out of His own nature. This we apprehend by faith. It is not an answer in the Q.E.D. sense, but it is an answer to live with and to live out. It is an act of faith in the best there is, or could be.

The other question, that of the two natures of man, is more bothersome in a practical way because it is closer to the ground. Its immediacy confronts us every day. St. Paul speaks to it when he writes, "For the good that I would I do not: but the evil which I would not, that I do" (Rom. 7:19). Bishop Jeremy Taylor wrote in the seventeenth century, "I am not a man, I am a civil war."

This is a problem familiar to all of us, the problem of *homo-duplex*. Between one's good intentions, with which hell is said to be paved, and the act itself there is apt to be a considerable distance. Why is this? If it is God who puts into our minds good desires why does He not make it more possible for the good desires to be fulfilled? The first given fact here is that God's will is good, freedom-making and constant. He does not constrain us, except by His inexhaustible loving-kindness, because such a constraint would mean that He was treating us as objects rather than persons. And He made us persons, with the possibility of acting against His will for us. In fact He supports us when we decide to choose against Him. We can have it that way if we want it that way and with God's permission.

Sometimes we wish that God were not (so we could be God) or that He would go away and stop bothering us. We want to be free and in this pursuit frequently forget that every man is in bondage to that which he loves most. This is true, as we have seen, of St. Paul's pilgimage; he travels a road all the way from bondage under the Law—the belief that he can attain righteousness by fulfilling commandments—to being the slave of Jesus Christ, in

47

whom he is *made* righteous but by God's act rather than his own—"whose service is perfect freedom."

Francis Thompson describes our flight from God in *The Hound of Heaven:*

> *I fled Him, down the nights and down the days;*
> *I fled Him, down the arches of the years;*
> *I fled Him, down the labyrinthine ways*
> *Of my own mind; and in the mist of tears*
> *I hid from Him, and under running laughter.*

Running away from god has been going on for a long time. Thompson's poem was written in 1893 when the poet was thirty-four years old. It is a perceptive and powerful description of the double nature of man and of the God who pursues him with the gift of his redemption. Some people think the poem is based on the singing lines of Psalm 139 which describes the same flight:

> *Whither shall I go then from thy Spirit?*
> *Or whither shall I go then from thy presence?*
> *If I climb up into heaven, thou art there;*
> *If I go down to hell, thou art there also.*
> *If I take the wings of the morning,*
> *And remain in the uttermost parts of the sea;*
> *Even there also shall thy hand lead me,*
> *And thy right hand shall hold me.*

These two poets, writing almost three thousand years apart, see the same struggle and come to the same conclusion; first, that no man can run away from God, and secondly, that God pursues us with only one weapon, His goodness and loving-kindness. St. Augustine, fourth-century Bishop of Hippo, writing just about midway between our two poets says, "Thou hast made us for Thyself, and our hearts are restless until they find their rest in Thee."

On the basis of the biblical record we seem to be faced with three considerations: that God is wholly good, that man is divided, that God accepts us on our own valuation while at the same time He offers us the possibility of wholeness in communion with Himself. The last consideration is illustrated in the parable of the Laborers and the Hours (Matt. 20:1–16). The familiar story tells of a man who goes out early in the morning to hire workers for his vineyard. This was day labor and he offers a denarius (about twenty cents in silver) which was the usual rate and acceptable to the workers. About nine o'clock and again about noon and at three, he hires on additional helpers and sends them to the vineyard. As the working day is about to end he finds some men in the market place still unemployed and hires them too.

When it comes time to pay off the help he gives each of them a denarius, no matter how many hours he has worked. This causes one of those who has worked all day to complain that he and his early companions have been unjustly dealt with. This is the man who is asking for his just deserts! The employer replies that he has dealt fairly; they agreed for a certain sum and they got it. If he chooses to pay the others at the same rate, whose business is that but his own? "Is it not lawful for me to do what I will with mine own?" This is where the parable ends.

Jesus tells this story about the kingdom of heaven to which the vineyard and its owner are likened. It is not a business story about how to run a vineyard profitably but a story about our eternal relationship with God and about His goodness and loving-kindness to us and to all men. It does not mean that an employer can do anything he pleases with his own property, nor does it attempt to make rules for wage scales; but God can do as He pleases because He is the ultimate owner of all things. And what He pleases is to have all men in loving relationship with Him. This is what the kingdom of heaven is.

The parable is illuminating in our inquiry into man's divided nature and God's attitude toward us. It says rather plainly that if we want a contract with God we can have it, but that will be the end of it. "Friend, I am doing you no wrong: did you not agree with me for a denarius? Take what belongs to you, and go." If that is the way we define our relationship with God, He will accept our definition and treat us justly. But He is ready to give more than we desire or deserve, not on the basis of any merit or on our part, but because of His own nature. God is not an employer, He is a giver of gifts.

It follows from this that our hope of wholeness is in response to God's generosity toward us—the thanksgiving of ourselves in acts large and small, strong and feeble to the good God who loves us and (even more remarkable) continues to love us, in spite of ourselves.

Again, to look at the biblical record as a whole, we can see that the growing, developing understanding of the nature of God always goes hand in hand with a widening and deepening of concern for all of God's creation. When men thought of God chiefly as a tribal deity their sympathies ended where the tribe ended. But there is the beginning of the concept that God personally involves Himself in the affairs of men. The fifth chapter of the book of Judges—the Song of Deborah—is a magnificent piece of folk poetry; savage, eloquent and utterly devoted to the interests of the group of tribes over whom their God presides at the expense of their enemies. As this nation grows in size and power and self-consciousness its people are tempted to forget their God and to believe in themselves. Frequently they do so. Again and again the prophets, the seers, speak forth in the name of God to recall the people to the things that belong to their peace. In the eighth century B.C. when the hotheads of the land wanted to make an alliance with Egypt against the Assyrian conqueror Sennacherib, Isaiah the prophet warned, "The Egyptians are men, and not God; and their horses flesh, and not spirit. In returning and rest shall ye be saved; in quietness and in confidence shall be your strength: and ye would not" (Isa. 31:3, 30:15),

God is always willing to give us more than we want to receive. We want to do it ourselves out of our pride. And just as it is a struggle for any individual to learn that other people have rights and privileges so we learn slowly that our well-being is bound up with the well-being of all men. It is "our" Father who art in heaven, not "mine." The Bible contemplates the redemption of all men and all nature.

But as God is alive in history, maker of all things and judge of all men, so is He alive in the personal history of every man. "Surely the Lord is loving into every man," even when no one else seems to be. "Surely thy loving-kindness and mercy shall follow me all the days of my life," when nothing else but trouble seems to follow me. This is not always easy to see, especially at a time when things are going wrong. But looking backward through the arches of the years, one knows himself to have been sustained, guided and refreshed. We know this through the eye of faith, but faith itself is a gift of God's loving-kindness. We do not invent it, we receive it.

Having received God's goodness which is poured out on all mankind, we become responsible for what we have knowingly received. Jesus tells us that if we have a quarrel with our brother it is our first responsibility to make peace with him before we come to make an offering in church. We cannot "love our enemies" in the large with any honesty if we have not made an attempt at reconciliation with the "enemies" close at hand. The end of that road would be to "give thanks for all men"—that absurd and haunting phrase! It might also be a world at peace instead of a world in fear.

The opposite of receiving God's goodness and giving it away takes many familiar forms. Losing one's temper, for instance—a literal statement. When a blade loses its temper it loses its integrity, its usefulness as a blade. So with ourselves. We momentarily become less than ourselves in the solitary confinement of our own anger. And, impractical as it may sound, the only medicine for it is thanksgiving. Again, let me illustrate. Some years ago in New York City a young man agreed to try his hand at running a boys' club, under church auspices, in one of the seamier neighborhoods of the city. He was an intelligent young man, full of good will toward his new charges, and brimming with plans. But, try as he might, he could not get through to a certain boy in the group. The boy was bright enough but he seemed possessed of the devil. Whatever the plan was and however well thought out in advance, this boy seemed able to ruin it simply by being there. After a number of frustrating Saturdays the young man in charge finally blew up. He told the boy exactly what he thought of him, fired him out of the club and told him never to come back! The boy, who seemed to be really impressed for the first time, departed. And he did not come back.

A week or two later the young man, a bit ashamed of his outburst and pursued by his conscience, looked the boy up at the address he had given. It turned out to be a grubby and forbidding tenement and the boy the oldest of several children. His father was dead, a victim of the

Prohibition wars, his mother a charwoman in an office building. The spurned boy was making some attempt to take care of two younger children and received his caller with surprise and not a little hostility. But the young man, having taken in the surroundings, was moved with amazement and thankfulness that the boy was as good as he was. That visit turned out to be a valuable one for both of them and the beginning of a new understanding, a new usefulness.

Familiar to all of us is another form of refusing God's loving-kindness, that of dodging responsibility—"let George do it." There is an old story of a harvest festival in an Italian village which tells it well. It was the local custom for a large cask to be set up in the market place at harvest time and to this common store each farmer would contribute a measure of wine from his own grapes. The story goes that a certain farmer, feeling that his own yield had been so meager that he could not afford to make the customary offering, decided on a subterfuge. He came to the market place with a wicker-covered jug filled with water, made conversation with the people standing about, and emptied his jug into the communal cask. He was present on the day of the festival when the citizens gathered to make holiday and drink the product of their common labor. But when the governor of the feast turned the spigot on the cask nothing came out but pure water!

Turning the story around we see that it may be our own contribution, perphaps one which seems to us insignificant, which makes a large enterprise possible. What is involved here is the whole idea of Christian community. It is doubtless true that the Church cannot bear its witness in the world without competent leadership but it is also true that such leadership would come to nothing without the support of devoted and unspectacular people behind the scenes. The key would seem to be the willing-ness of many people, large and small, to respond in thank-ful self-giving to the goodness of God, each in terms of his own gifts. The rewards of God are not quantitative. He gives of Himself to each of us with an open hand. Our responsibility, indeed our privilege and our self-realization, lies in a thankful response to what we have been given. The whole missionary outreach of the Church has no other motive but to give away that which has been re-ceived from a loving God.

The giving of gifts is as old as mankind and the meaning of the gift as various as human motives. A gift may be given in hostility or in revenge as well as in gratitude. A present may be a "white elephant" and an embarrassment. A gift may be a sop distributed casually, as a political bone to a dog. A gift may be given as an obligation in a vague sort of way, like some Christmas presents, or in an automatic sort of way because of social custom. Gifts have been offered to placate the gods, to buy off enemies, to curry favor, to soften up prospective customers, to sym-bolize success. But all of these and any others, however good, fade into nothingness against God's gift of Himself, His goodness and loving-kindness poured out without condition on the children of men.

God is unlimited but we are limited. God has all the time there is, all eternity. We have only the time we have been given, the "sacrament of the passing moment," the way in which we may enter into the eternity of God. Daily, God blesses us with His goodness. Our meaning as persons, the possibility of our own goodness, lies in the quality of our response to His goodness and loving-kind-ness to us, and to all men.

V

. . . We bless Thee
for our creation, preservation, and
all the blessings of this life . . .

We did not ask to be born. There may be times when we regret that it happened though few, perhaps, would go so far as to say with Jeremiah in a moment of bitterness, "Cursed be the day wherein I was born." And while there have always been those who have taken their own lives, and probably always will be, most of us prefer to keep on living as long as possible. The real question here is the quality of the living. The spectrum of response runs all the way from the feeble thread of life desperately held on to in the concentration camp in the face of cold and starvation and brutality, to the pulsing vitality of a man strong and free and in love with life. There are many who seem to keep on living more from force of habit than anything else. There are those who discover much later than others the satisfactions of living. There are those who wish that they had their lives to live over again and those who live more than one life at a time. At the most, life seems exciting and rewarding and full of adventure. At the least, it seems a better thing than the absence of it.

At any rate we have been blessed with it and, in this prayer, we bless God for giving it to us. Before we think any more about our own lives we might ask ourselves, why life at all? Why creation? Why did it all begin in the first place?

And before plunging in for an answer to that question we shall have to decide what symbols to adopt, what sort of pictorial language we are going to use. In general we have to decide to look at the universe either as Greeks or as Hebrews. The former, the scientific approach, has occupied the dominant place in the imagination of Europeans and Americans for the past two hundred years. We have become increasingly scientific in our way of looking at things and defining them. It is a good tool, a good method, by which we have discovered many new things about the world we live in. It is a good way to measure things and to test them and to determine their uses and limitations. We are sometimes tempted to say that so and so is not a *fact* unless it can be demonstrated by the scientific method. What this leads to, of course, is a secular view of the world, the one-story universe. What it leaves out is the meaning of things and events. An exact physical description of the mechanics of the playing of a violin sonata might be interesting, even important, but it would not necessarily convey the meaning or the benefit of the music played.

So with this created world. To say that we live in a universe that can be measured, described and predicted is true (and useful) but it is not the whole truth. The biblical insight and lived-out experience, the other interpretation, is that God, acting "on His own motion," creates the universe for a purpose. He is alive in the events of history. He presides over the destinies of men and nations. He is the ground of being, the author of freedom. And in this universe is poetry and mystery and terror and fulfillment.

John Donne, the greatest of the seventeenth-century religious poets, says in a sermon:

Had God company enough of himselfe; was he satisfied in the *three Persons?* We see he proceeded further; he came to a *Creation;* And as soon as he had made *light* (which was his first Creature) he took a pleasure in it; he said *it was good;* he was glad of it; glad of the *Sea,* glad of the *Earth,* glad of the *Sunne,* and *Moone,* and *Starres,* and he said of every one, *It is good;* . . .

The question comes up again, why did God make man? Or in different words, why did God allow man to become himself, a creature possessed of self-knowledge, self-consciousness, self-will? We can only guess at an answer, and that only on the basis of analogous predication—that is, by thinking of what we ourselves would do and then enlarging it. Like this. Consider yourself alone in a primitive world, like the world of Adam in the mind of the writer of the book of Genesis. Having acquired clothing and shelter and food, what would you want next? Someone to share it with, someone to talk to—probably about the weather—companionship.

Here is the paradox. God does not need anything in order to be Himself; He is whole. He certainly does not need *us*. But the other side of the paradox is that God, because He is the God revealed in the biblical drama of creation and redemption, because He is this kind of God, created an object of His love. This is man, who is beloved of God and capable of loving God in return. The history of mankind, and the meaning of the history, is the story of that relationship.

There are parts of this story that we are never going to understand while we are on pilgrimage. We do "see through a glass darkly" or, as J. B. Phillips puts it, "We are like men looking at a landscape in a small mirror." There are a good many things we do not have to understand. Albert Schweitzer says that our highest knowledge is to know that we are surrounded by a mystery. But it is not a mystery that baffles and frustrates and irritates; rather, it is a part of an accepted reality that we are citizens of two worlds, that we are permitted to live in time and eternity at once. The creature is made, the Creator *is*.

Constance Carrier has caught this two-worlds theme sensitively in a poem about a child called Lisa:

> *Under the great down-curving lilac branches,*
> *a dome of coolness and a cave of bloom,*
> *Lisa, vague-eyed, chin-propped, cross-legged is sitting*
> *within a leaf-walled room.*
>
> *Beyond the curtaining green, her brothers wrangle,*
> *cars pass, a huckster shouts, a bicycle bell*
> *is brisk, is brief, dogs bark. She does not hear them.*
> *She is netted in silence, she is lost in a spell.*
>
> *She has chosen to come here, but she is not hiding,*
> *nor in disgrace, nor sulky. She is alone*
> *of her free will—alone and yet not lonely:*
> *this quarter hour her own.*

She could not tell you herself what she is thinking,
or what she makes of this kingdom she has found.
Presently she will go and join the others:
her voice will sound

with theirs. But now the candid light, come sifting
thro leaves, illuminates another view.
O leaf and light, that can divide thus cleanly
the world in two

and give the halves to a child, so to acquaint her
with the mind's need of quietude for growth,
yet interpose no barrier between them,
that she may move in both.

The familiar scene of the Transfiguration of Christ is the biblical picture of this truth in religious terms (Lk. 9:28–36). Jesus, taking with him Peter and James and John, goes up into a mountain and there, while he is praying, the disciples get a glimpse of who he really is. The passage occurs in an earlier version in St. Mark (9:2–10). What is being said is that for a brief moment the dark glass becomes clear and three ordinary men see all the way through into eternity, perceiving the Messiahship of Jesus in glory. The door does sometimes open, more often than not in the midst of quite ordinary events and associations, lighting up the mind in a kind of rapid flash never to be forgotten or lost.

The sequel to the Transfiguration story is equally illuminating (Lk. 9:37–43a, Mk. 9:14–27). Coming down from the mountain Jesus is met by a crowd of people, among them a man who begs him to heal his epileptic boy whom the disciples have been unable to help. The boy is restored to health. The glory of the Lord is not a detached glory; it is involved in the griefs of the world, the anguish of men.

Thanks Be To God

There is a delightful story from G. K. Chesterton's early writing days which has to do with the encounter of an Oxford undergraduate with his tutor. The tutor, a bright young man and a follower of the pessimistic views of Schopenhauer, had a particular aversion to the exhibits of middle-class dreariness which could be seen from the windows of his second-floor lodgings. Chief among these offenses was a desperately unattractive stucco house and a silly duck pond complete with ducks. At the end of one of his frequent observations on the foolishness of people, the low estate of most human minds and the futility of life in general, the tutor concluded that the only intelligent course of action for a man of sense and sensibility would be to remove himself from the scene permanently.

The undergraduate considered this. He was a large and matter-of-fact young man, not much given to theorizing, and he decided the time had come to put the matter to a test. So he returned after one of the tutorial sessions, brandishing a wicked-looking revolver, and declared that he had come to put his tutor out of his misery! Reduced at once to unphilosophical entreaties the poor man, begging for his life, retreated out of the window and perched precariously on the flagpole where he hoped to attract the attention of passers-by to his plight. In this position (the large undergraduate sitting in the window waving the revolver while the tutor rode his insubstantial rail) the former devotee of pessimism was called upon to recant. He was asked to give thanks for his miserable life, for the sky, the earth, the trees. He was given opportunity to bless his neighbors, to overlook the deficiencies of their taste in architecture, even to express his satisfaction at the ducks on the pond! So the battle ended and the tutor came back to life.

What do we value most? Life, certainly, and its continuance. What else? Well, most of us value certain *things*

—useful things, beautiful things, sentimental things, handy things. It is interesting to speculate about what armful of things we would take from our own house if we had to leave it suddenly, knowing that we would never return. It is especially difficult when one is no longer young and over the years has gathered a number of household treasures.

Beyond these things, many of which convey deep meaning to us, there are the priceless and measureless intangibles. There is the trust of one's own child, a gift not to be bought or bargained for. There is the taste of a fine morning, food when we are hungry, the stretch of useful labor, sleep when we are tired. There is the good opinion of one's associates, the joy of companionship, the wonder and forbearance and healing of love. There is the dignity of being a man. These are good and of God. They cannot be paid for except sometimes in kind and in a life lived out in thankfulness. These are gifts of our creation and preservation, and they are accepted (or not) from moment to moment as they are offered.

One of our illusions is that we can go back and make up somehow for a time passed, an offering missed. In his philosophical travel diary, *An Inland Voyage,* Robert Louis Stevenson again gives us true and graceful words. Floating down the Oise with another young man (this was in 1878 when the author was twenty-eight) in two canoes, they are hospitably received in the town of Origny. In fact they cause quite a local stir. When they come to leave, a number of the young people of the town, with four girls in the lead, run along the bank of the stream calling, "Come back! Come back!" Soon the river whisks them around a turn and they are gone. The author writes:

Come back? There is no coming back, young ladies, on the impetuous stream of life.

Thanks Be To God

The merchant bows unto the seaman's star,
The ploughman from the sun his season takes.

And we must all set our pocket watches by the clock of
fate. There is a headlong, forthright tide, that bears away
man with his fancies like a straw, and runs fast in time and
space. It is full of curves like this, your winding river of
the Oise; and lingers and returns in pleasant pastorals; and
yet, rightly thought upon, never returns at all. For though
it should revisit the same acre of meadow in the same hour,
it will have made an ample sweep between whiles; many
little streams will have fallen in; many exhalations risen
towards the sun; and even although it were the same acre,
it will no more be the same river of Oise. And thus, O
graces of Origny, although the wandering fortune of my
life should carry me back again to where you await death's
whistle by the river, that will not be the old I who walks
the street; and those wives and mothers, say, will those be
you?

There is no going back. The man who revisits his old
home town after a number of years is usually disappointed.
The trees are not as tall, the houses not as grand, the
streets not as wide as he remembered them. He is looking
for a boy who does not live there any more; in a sense he
never did live there, he was just passing through. The
stream flows only one way.

The other illusion, as old as time, is that we can run
away. When the going gets rough, when we are unsuccess-
ful or unappreciated, we can take the "geographical cure"
and find greener pastures. The trouble is, of course, that
when we run we take ourselves with us for no man can
run away from himself.

There may be good reason for going—the desire to
look on new scenes of strangeness and wonder.

Thanks Be To God

I should like to rise and go
Where the golden apples grow.

And, as several of our greatest writers have taught us, some of the richest travel is done in the kingdom of the imagination.

The key is the ability to look on scenes, new or old, with fresh eyes. A woman once complained to a French landscape painter, "I can't see in nature the things you put in your pictures," to which he replied, "But don't you wish you could?"

We have been given our life, our times, our world as a gift of God. Each age has its own problems to itself. Among our own are the tensions and bewilderments of a rapidly expanding universe and the struggle of a man to be a man in a mechanical world. But the root fact remains that life and time are God's gifts, even in a late industrial society. This is all the time we have. Yesterday is gone, tomorrow never comes. The time is Now, God's eternity on a clock. We have been preserved for this hour.

Consider the miracle of a day. All night long the pulse of the earth beats slowly in the darkness. Country places, following the rhythm of the soil, have gone to bed early while in cities there is a life native to the night: the watchman going his rounds, the world of entertainment, the policeman walking his beat, the night nurse, the baker, the night editor at work on the morning paper. But it feels like night. Tomorrow means daylight.

There comes a wind before the dawn, tossing ships at their moorings, sighing through New England pine woods as day flies the Atlantic. Light spreads and rises, paling the stars and giving back to bay and headland their familiar outlines. Farms and villages begin to stir, alarm clocks jangle in thousands of city bedrooms in a procession of sound as the day moves westward. Life begins again. The sky is full of promise. Then the sun rises, sending long level heralds of light before it, and the day has begun. Nothing has happened in it yet. It is clean, unspoiled, unwritten on, fresh-minted from the hand of God. To some it will be a burden, to many just another day. To those who bless God for their creation, preservation and all the blessings of this life it will be a gift. "This is the day which the Lord has made; we will rejoice and be glad in it."

Creation is continuous because God is alive in what He has made. There is a phrase common in educational circles, "creative activity." It usually describes a class or group when the children are encouraged to use their imagination. But the phrase actually describes an attribute of God, whose creative activity is the source of imagination and artistry and design. When a man makes something in his home workshop, something that was not there yesterday, it is genuine creation, an aspect of God's creative activity. So it is with a new idea which spurs and illuminates, or with the making of a poem, a statue, a garden. God's creativity is involved. When a woman has a baby it is just as much a miracle as the first day of creation, just as new.

The greatest blessings of this life are personal blessings. It is said of the publisher, Thomas Nelson, that he improved situations by living in them. Most of us have known a few people like that who have widened our views and enriched our understanding. Most of us have known the joys and satisfactions of friendship, through which God offers to us His involvement with us. Most of us have known the giving and receiving of love through which we enter into the creativity of God, and into our preservation. Love from God, learned by us slowly through the people of God, heals, sustains and makes new.

Love seems to be available in three general varieties. The one which comes to us most easily is self-love. The current exhibit of this says, "I am the master of my [scientific] fate" and the end of it is chaos. Then there is goodness-by-contract, my rights ("Lo, these many years do I serve thee"). This is life imprisonment. Finally, there is the glad response to God's love in Christ through the people of God in thanksgiving. This is eternal life and, therefore, the right use of time and people and things here and now.

VI

*. . . but above all,
for thine inestimable love
in the redemption of the world
by our Lord Jesus Christ . . .*

Central to the Christian faith is the belief that Jesus Christ,
truly man and truly God, is the savior of mankind from
eternal death to eternal life. This is the heart of Christian
theology and the focal point of the General Thanksgiving.
The first half of the prayer leads up to it, the second
half derives from it. Before we consider the fact of salvation itself it might be helpful to raise the questions, Saved
from what? and to *to* what?

This involves us, of course, in the problem of evil.
There seem to be three sorts or types of evil that we can
observe around us and in us and while they overlap they

are sufficiently different so we can talk about them a little. The first of these we might call natural evil; it has no moral quality, no ill will but can be a background against which moral qualities, both good and bad, are displayed. An example here might be a natural public disaster such as a flood or an earthquake or a forest fire. The event is neither good nor bad by intent, it is simply there. Deaths and accidents and lootings may take place because of it, taking advantage of it, but so may rescues and sacrifices and acts of kindness. No *thing* in itself has any moral quality. A dollar bill as such is neither good nor bad. You may cut a cord of wood with an ax, or you can kill your brother with it. It is the same ax. The goodness or badness of the action lies not in the ax but in the will of the person using it. One may have doubts about the judgment of people who choose to live on the slopes of an active volcano or in a river valley which is swept by disastrous floods year after year, but few would think that in such a case the volcano or the river was out to get them.

The second type of evil is more difficult to describe. It has been called a number of things, among them original sin. It is the pull backward with which each of us is born, the bias in our own behalf, our self-love. This is not a theory (though it has many theoretical explanations) but a condition to be accepted and, if possible, dealt with. It has been noted that if one watches children at play one can see elements of every political philosophy except demcoracy—and the one out in front and running strong is fascism!

In its milder forms this tendency is represented by self-deception and self-protection. We sometimes decide to believe what we want to believe in the face of any sort of evidence. And it is with the greatest gentleness that we break the bad news about ourselves. Or it may take the form of excessive self-assertiveness. A young woman once described her mother as the sort of person who goes through life "asking to see the manager"! At the other end of the scale this tendency means self-destruction. Each of us has within himself the seeds of his own destruction. Sometimes we insist upon it.

There is a mystery here. Often we do not know why we do the things we do, things we did not even intend so far as we know. In recent times, helped by the new sciences of psychology and psychiatry, we have come to know many useful and some disturbing things about our motives and our unconscious desires. But the mystery remains. We are shocked when we read newspaper reports of acts of wantonness and violence, done with no apparent reason at all. I remember an incident of a number of years ago, in a New England fall, when I was raking and burning leaves. Several neighborhood children gathered to watch the fire and to help poke it. Soon the fire got very hot, widening the circle of children. A little girl clutched a rag doll, the doll itself a neighborhood character, while she stood watching. Suddenly a boy about the same age snatched the doll from her arms and tossed it into the heart of the blaze. I grabbed the little girl to keep her from going in after it and in a moment the doll was no more. The boy's older sister, her face white with shock, turned to her brother and demanded in a tight voice, "John, why did you do that?" The boy said nothing, just shrugged his shoulders and walked away. He himself did not know why. One might make some guesses. A competent person might get close to an explanation, but the mystery of evil remains. And when one is no longer a child it still remains. There are no nice people who are incapable of doing blazingly stupid and destructive things.

Jeremiah wrote, "The heart is deceitful above all things,
. . . who can know it?" (17:9).

The third type of evil familiar to us is evil which is
deliberately chosen. This is sin, actual sin, which always
involves a choice. It has three marks. First, it is an act
against conscience. A sinful act is one decided upon
against oneself, against one's better judgment, against
one's knowledge of the good. There is always a strain, unless one has persisted so long in a sinful course of action
that it does not hurt any more and choice is automatic.
That would be moral disease and it is frightening in its
power. Probably the most completely villainous character
in English letters is Shakespeare's Iago who represents the
pursuit of evil for evil's sake.

The second mark of sin is that it sets out to build a
private world which is different from the one God made.
While original sin is the tendency to be God, to play God,
actual sin puts it into practice. In the parable of the
Prodigal Son (really the Prodigal Father, who loves both
sons) each boy builds his private world, unrelated to the
one the father offers. The younger son's world is in his
imagination and, briefly, in a far country. He "comes to
himself," repents, comes home and is restored. The elder
boy's private world is in his own self-righteousness which
he refuses to leave.

Thirdly, sin is not so much an infraction of a law as it is
a blow at a loving heart. It is a violation of trust since
only those who trust us are open to be struck. If a boy
sins in a small way against his mother the hard thing to
face is not punishment—he could take that and still keep
his dignity. The hard thing to face is mother's loving eye.
So it was when "the Lord turned, and looked upon Peter"
(Lk. 22:61), for sin is always an offense against God.

We begin to see the nature of man's predicament. He

is man against himself, trapped by his self-love, involved in a sinful society, unable to save himself, to forgive himself, to deliver himself. And at the same time he catches glimpses of what he might be, of usefulness, of freedom to choose wisely. It is as if he were at the bottom of a deep and slippery well. He can see the sky and know the sun is shining on the earth but he is unable to get to it. Being intelligent will not do it, nor will good intentions or promises. He is stuck and unless help comes from outside in the form of someone ready, willing and able to help, he will continue to be stuck.

This is the reason for what Christians call the Incarnation, the coming of the God-man, Jesus the Christ, into the midst of our trouble. There was no other way for God, being God, to meet the problem. Consider what happened and continues to happen, since all of the actions of God are continuous. Everyman (this is what Adam means) is created free and given everything that he needs. He exchanges his freedom for the bondage of more knowledge than he can handle, because he wants to be God. He does this whether in the Garden of Eden or in Philadelphia or Sioux Falls. He reveals himself.

In response God reveals Himself, as the same God who made the world and who made man as an object of His love, because it is His nature to be loving. This is the parallel to the act of creation. When things had gone terribly wrong, with Everyman caught in a maze of his own making, God presumably could have written off the whole experiment as a mistake. But this would have been a violation of His own nature. Or, presumably, He could have raised us all to a higher state of being, but only by treating persons as objects—as things, without the possibility of growth or of self-realization. This too would have been an act against His own nature as well as against man's nature.

There was (and is) only one thing left for God to do and that is to come Himeslf, with personal involvement and at personal expense. Someone has said that he has always admired God for not sending a committee!

The length to which God is willing to go is indicated by the expense and shame of the Cross. "Ye are bought with a price" (1 Cor. 6:20). God's love for us is measureless and absurd by our standards. When Jesus on the cross says, and keeps on saying, "Father forgive them; for they know not what they do," he is saying it in the face of everything the world has to throw—hatred and malice, jealousy and anger and pride and indifference. We were represented there. We are there now. And so is God, giving Himself away.

Soon after I moved into the house where I now live I began to have conversations every once in a while with one of my new neighbors, a girl of about eight whose name was Emily. Walking home one day I came to Emily's house where she was sitting on the front step. I stopped to say hello and was about to leave when she said, "What do people preach about in your church?" I replied that they preach about the best things they know. "What," she asked, "is the best thing you know?" I turned the question back, "What is the best thing *you* know?" She considered it gravely and finally answered, "I think the best thing is to have a friend." I agreed. I still do—"Who for us men and for our salvation came down from heaven."

Out of World War II came a story—one of the by-products of tragedy—which carries this truth one more step and brings it into sharp focus. This is the story of a fighter pilot who was shot down over Germany and spent nine months in a German prison camp. He was describing his experience to a friend of his and told how in his training days he was instructed in the use of a parachute, but had never actually used one. Things happened fast in the war at that time and he was never given an opportunity to bail out. He was shipped overseas. Then a desperate moment came in combat over Germany. Surrounded by enemy fighter planes his own plane was hit and burst into flames. He knew he had to jump. He did, but he could not pull the ripcord at once because the enemy planes were too close. So he had to fall free, waiting until he came to a cloud bank before pulling the cord. His friend, both impressed and curious, said, "I don't see how you could do it, never having done it before." The ex-pilot said, "I could do it because I knew it was my only chance."

This is what the Christian faith teaches about the meaning of Christ. When Peter, arrested by the temple police for preaching "through Jesus," stood up to address his accusers, he held up before them the Lord Christ whom they had nailed to a cross and whom God had raised from the dead. As he presented the truth of Christ to them he added the phrase, "He is our only chance," or in the actual words of Peter, "There is salvation in no one else" (Acts 4:12).

Or look at another picture, one common to our experience. Consider a child lost in the woods. He has wandered off from the family camping place to pick berries or follow the flight of a bird or just to wander. The world is a pleasant place and new adventures beckon around every bend. Bees buzz in flower cups, butterflies flicker through the air in flashes of color. Time stands still.

He enters the woods scarcely knowing that he is doing so. Slowly the friendly world begins to darken and he finds himself in strange territory. Time comes back and it is later than he thought. The trees are huge and menacing, briers pluck at his clothes. He stops and looks around him. Every place looks like every other place; he is not even sure how he came here. There is no sound except the wind, faint and high up in the tops of trees. He cries out, uncertainly, but no sound comes back. He is lost. Fear tightens in his stomach. He crouches miserably at the foot of a tree and begins to cry.

Now the child's father misses him and having looked in the likely places near home without seeing him, sets out to find him. To the father the trees are not menacing, they are just trees. The forest gloom does not frighten him as he walks along calling for his son. Presently he hears an answering cry, "I'm over here." ("Here I am," says Abraham, Jacob, Moses, Samuel, Isaiah.) With quick strides the boy is found, gathered into the father's arms and safe. The father laughs at the joy of finding his lost son. In his relief the boy says little or nothing but he knows he is on the way home, held by a strength larger than his own. He can afford not to be afraid any more.

This is the story of mankind, "lost in a haunted wood," and this is the story of salvation. "The Son of man is come to seek and to save that which was lost" (Lk. 19:10).

Take one more modern parable. A boy sets out to make an impression on a little girl. As natural man, flexing his muscles and trying to look adequate, he casts about for a suitable stage on which to display his prowess. This is a city boy and he settles for the brick-ornamented corner of a three-floor apartment house. Against future need he has already made a note of this possibility—a very easy climb as a matter of fact, but impressive enough to the impressionable. So he starts up on rubber-soled shoes, climbing with just enough apparent difficulty to produce the desired response in his audience.

All goes well with natural man, junior grade. He climbs farther and farther from the solid earth, up the dizzy slopes of ambition. The little girl makes satisfying noises of admiration and alarm. Then it happens. He comes to the top where the roof overhangs and he is stuck. He can't get over the edge of the roof and he can't climb down because he can't see where to put his feet. All his self-importance evaporated, he is a little boy in a highly nervous state and badly in need of help. This is the state of natural man; where he is that he would not, where he would that he is not.

Natural woman below, her hero reduced to unheroic proportions, goes into action. Calling to the boy to hold on she runs off to find her father who is a house painter and breathlessly explains why he must come at once. The painter does so unenthusiastically, bringing a ladder from the job. They converge upon the boy, who is hugging the bricks with his knees and wishing he were almost anywhere else. He cries to them to hurry.

The ladder goes up and the painter climbs it, calling encouragement to the boy. There comes the difficult moment when the boy has to let go his relatively safe hold on the bricks, even though he is about at the end of his endurance, and give himself in an act of faith to this stranger who will lift him through the empty air to the ladder. It is finished. The boy is on the ground again, his salvation wrought.

Most of the elements are here, our pride, our self-display, our "fall," our rescue because of the compassionate involvement of God in Christ. Missing only is the extremity of that involvement, the death on the cross that we might be free. This happened once and for all in God's ultimate response to man's need, and it is true for all time.

Consider a man in middle life, married and the father of two or three children. He is an average citizen, nothing unusual. He has a job which interests him moderately and which pays his bills. He has a place in his community, a few good friends, a number of acquaintances. He has some life insurance, perhaps a retirement plan. He reads a little, looks at television a little, is mildly interested in the affairs of the world. He owns his home, an automobile, is in pretty good health. Soon the children will be married and move away. It is not a bad life but somehow it is not quite what he had planned, what he had hoped for. Something is missing from the middle of it. He does not think of himself as excited or eager about the years that lie ahead. The prospect looks like a general downward slope. He would not say that he feels sinful—the word would seem to him overdramatic—but he does sometimes feel frustrated, insignificant, a bit lonely, occasionally bored. There is a certain drying up of the vital sap, a fading of an earlier dream.

This man (his name is legion) needs help. But what kind? More money would not be the answer, not a deep or a lasting one; nor would a different job or a different wife or a different place in which to live. It is not the outside that needs changing but the inside. He thinks about it once in a while, then gives it up as unanswerable. "That's life," he says.

Now consider the good news of the Gospel. News, not advice. Not pious phrases or uplift or vague promises of pie in the sky or inspiration. But the strange and wonderful news that the same God who made the world lived in the world, died, went through the grave and the gate of death and came out on the other side. And He is alive. It says that He died for our sins—for all of those frustrations, those accumulated self-defeats, those countless choices against the best we know—in order that we might be free. He is strong to save—from anything, in spite of anything, in the face of anything. And this saving is for all men at all times, in all places. It is offered in companionship, the good companionship that makes all other companionship meaningful, including that of a man with himself. This is the new life in Christ that makes it possible for a man to die in peace, whenever and gladly. This is God's compassionate involvement in the life of men.

There is no place in the Gospel (God's spiel, God talking through men) that lists the things we should give up in order to make ourselves pleasing to God. St. Paul makes catalogs both of positive and negative qualities (e.g. Rom. 12, Gal. 5:19–26) but a close look will discover that the good qualities are "fruits of the Spirit," that is, the results of accepting God's gift of new life in Christ, while the destructive qualities are the byproducts of having rejected God's offer of Himself. There is no way—no set of rules—whereby we can make ourselves morally desirable to God so He will have to accept us. The good news is much better than that. It says that God accepts us the way we are because of His nature, not our record and because of His generosity, our new life can begin. The operator here is God Himself in the person of Jesus Christ our Lord who makes himself known in the texture of history ("suffered under Pontius Pilate") and who reveals himself in the midst of our need.

This always involves a choice on our part since God does not coerce us. When the rich man came to Jesus asking how he might inherit eternal life (Mk. 10:17–22) and explained in answer to a question that he had kept all the commandments from his youth up, Jesus said to him, "One thing thou lackest; go thy way, sell whatsoever thou hast, and give to the poor, and thou shalt have treasure in heaven; and come, . . . follow me." The story goes on to say that the man (St. Matthew calls him a young man) went away "sorrowful." He almost did it! This does not mean that it is wrong to be rich, though the rich man has temptations and responsibilities which the poor man does not have; rather, it means that it is wrong to trust in riches because that is idolatry.

So it is with all of the other alternatives to God's gift of freedom—freedom to be, to choose, to become. Secretly, we want a prize for being good. *The* prize, *the* goodness, is the new life in Christ for which He pays, which He makes possible and which He offers without calculation. This is God's "inestimable love in the redemption of the world by our Lord Jesus Christ."

Centuries ago St. Augustine wrote, "So He who was God was made man, by taking what He was not, not by losing what He was: thus was God made man."

God made man,
God was made man,
God, made man, made man free.

VII

*. . . for the means of grace, and
for the hope of glory . . .*

I remember a piece of dialogue from a play some years
ago, a scrap of conversation between two persons at a
house party.

"Are you saved?"

"Yes."

"So am I. Isn't it nice!"

Salvation is a large-sized word, so much so that it can
mean nothing at all. One of the keys to understanding
it, I think, is to know that it describes a state of aliveness
rather than a situation (however pleasant) which is static.
One is saved *from* something and *for* something. The end
of it is not so much a sense of placid well-being as it is
a present fact of rightness restored, of direction found,
of willing involvement accepted. It is sometimes risky

and frequently expensive to receive; it is always expensive for God, the giver. One is saved by the power of God from the necessity of one's own self-destruction. Our place is taken by the Universal Man, God in Christ, who in so doing makes us free again. What we are saved for is life with God and in God and with any other person.

To apprehend this aspect of Christian belief requires an act of faith, since it takes some believing, but this act of faith is a part of the risk that many are not willing to take. For instance, here are some words from a letter written by an educated man in his middle forties:

. . . Self-love, yes. But so-called love of others is a myth, an illusion, often a cruelty. Love of children, especially one's own, is a ceremony of self-love and self-projection. Married "love" is a combination of sexual gratification and the security of knowing another person's habits and ways and customary reactions. So-called love of God is a meaningless cry for help to an unknown and unknowable; another form of self-love which fondly supposes that God, if He exists, is interested in the fact that I have a pain or can't pay the rent.

This is a self-love letter, written by a man who has posted "No Admittance" signs on all the doors to his inner being. He is not going to take the chance of being hurt by letting anybody in, including God. So he takes refuge in being smart enough to figure things out and to sound pretty clever about it. But it has a tinny sound. In disposing of God he shuts the door in his own face. The remarkable thing is that God has not disposed of *him!*

In a women's college parish I once received a delegation of students who wanted translations of some of the classical words of the Christian faith into ordinary speech. Among the entries was the word "grace" and we decided to start with it. The meaning of "graceful" was explored and agreed upon, after which we dug down to "gracious" which is not as easy to define. I asked these girls to characterize the gracious hostess at a dinner party. One of them suggested that at such a party, presided over by a gracious hostess, no one would wish he had not come. If he had worn the wrong clothes, for instance, he would be put at his ease and made to feel a member of the party. Another girl suggested that if one of the guests did something awkward, like spilling gravy on the table-cloth, the gracious hostess would be supportive, quick to repair the damage and to put the guest at ease. Then one of the students spoke a line which has stayed in my mind ever since. She said, "The gracious hostess stoops to help." What a window on the grace of God, "Who for us men and for our salvation came down from heaven!"

This is what the Christian doctrine of grace says. We cannot have innocence—we swapped that for apples a long time ago—but we can be restored by a gracious God who is willing to take the trouble. So our salvation is the result of God's grace, His compassionate involvement in the fumbling awkwardness, the pointless self-seeking, the isolating arrogance that each of us knows so well. It is easy for us to love people who already love us but it is quite a different thing to maintain, even in our mind, good will toward one who bristles with hostility. We are always tempted to bristle right back.

That God should love any man is surprising, that He should love all men is more surprising and that He should continue to do so is the most surprising of all. But the Christian faith says much more than this; it says that God in Christ identifies with the man who hates Him (not only the self-preening writer of the letter but also with

Judas) and offers up that man's sins as His own. When we give thanks to God for His "inestimable love in the redemption of the world by our Lord Jesus Christ; for the means of grace, and for the hope of glory," we remember that fact and give thanks for that almost unbelievable expense of love. We also give thanks, the more so as we come to learn more of its meaning, for the companionship of the risen Lord on our journey. In no place is this better set forth than in the story of the walk to Emmaus which St. Luke records (24:13–35). Read the passage, then hear these words written half a century ago by a man of God for his people in the village church:

A.

"Two of them went that same day to a village called Emmaus, which was from Jerusalem about three-score furlongs, and they talked together of all these things which had happened." We can sympathise so thoroughly with their sadness and understand so fully their impatience. They were turning their backs upon Jerusalem, the city of their hopes, in blank despair. Jesus had promised so much. It seemed that He had failed. The third day had come and they had not seen Him. They had ventured so much. They were sure it had been He who should have redeemed Israel. But here was no redemption. They talked to one another sadly enough of their disappointment as they returned to a desolate home.

We ourselves so often reproduce that picture. Is it not so with us even at Eastertide? We had hoped so much of what this Lent should bring forth. In our own life we looked for such progress, and there are so many failures. Still the old difficulties remain. There is so little sense of deliverance. In our friends we looked for such happiness and such help, and there has been the unexpected illness, the inexplicable misunderstanding, the continued discouragement. In the Church we looked for such signs of the working of God's grace. And there has been such a lack of public witness, such lamentable evidence of the power of Satan and of the growth of sin. We are ready to turn our backs upon the Holy City. We thought it had been He who should have redeemed Israel. But there is no redemption, no sense of fellowship, no sign of power. We talk to one another sadly about it. Once there had been no hope. But Jesus has come into our life and roused us to such high ventures and made us glow with such a sense of nearness, and led us out to such sacrifices— and then, after all, we find ourselves deceived. We are prepared to give up and go back to the empty, dark, and desolate home of the past. How well we know that mood of impatience, that overwhelming sense of failure!

And then at the very moment of sadness Jesus Himself joins us. We know not that it is He. We open our hearts to our Companion and tell Him frankly of our disappointment. He longs to hear. He never interrupts. He hears us to the end. The very outpouring of our souls in such simple confidence is the beginning of better things. So Jesus listens to us in our sorrow. He asks for our confidence now, as He did on that Emmaus road. Jesus listens as we pray. What an incentive to a simpler habit of prayer! We speak into the listening ear of the Divine Companion Who walks with us along the way of life. How real, how natural, how frank must be the language of our prayers! We can trust Jesus to understand. The great thing is really to want to tell Him.

B.

Jesus listens that He Himself may speak. When the disciples had finished their story, Jesus began to teach. He took them just as they were, and began to build upon what was real and true to them. He took them back to the old prophecies on which their hope still rested. As He spoke, new light sparkled and flashed upon those mysterious words in which the sufferings of Messiah had been hinted. There was a depth of meaning there, which had not yet been fathomed. Ought not, then, the Christ to have suffered these things and so to have entered into His glory? Thus faith once more revived in the hearts of the disciples. Their hearts began to burn, as Jesus opened to them the scriptures which they loved.

It is so with ourselves also. Jesus listens, that He may speak. He takes us just where we are. Our faith has received a shock. We hardly know whom or what to trust. A friend has failed us. New learning has discredited what we had believed to be true. Uncertainty threatens to declare itself where all had seemed so steadfast and so sure. Unexpected, undeserved trouble has fallen upon us. We tell it all to Jesus. And He takes us back to the one thing which is true to us, the one friend whom we still trust, the one fact of life which we do understand, the one simple truth we can still confess. And upon that He builds. He shows us how much more is implied in the acceptance of that one truth than we had ever thought. Gradually upon that one rock of certainty He builds up the structure of a fuller faith. Upon reality He can always build. We need just the courage to be real, the readiness to accept the full consequences of what we do believe, the faith to push to its logical sequel the truth which we have been able to understand. So Jesus teaches and our faith returns.

C.

And now the way is prepared for a new revelation of Jesus. Faith had returned as the disciples listened to His glowing words, and when He would pass on, they constrained Him to stay. Assuredly but for that loving constraint, He had not stayed. Then in the wonder of that homely meal, as He took the bread in His pierced Hands and blessed it in the familiar way, He was made known to them. He stood revealed as Jesus. And even in the very moment of recognition He vanished from their sight. It was enough. Jesus was alive. Jesus was with them, unseen but ever present. Their faith was strong enough now to receive the truth of His invisible Companionship. Through the gathering darkness of the night, the disciples returned alone to bear their joyful news to the Apostles at Jerusalem, whom they had left in such despair.

So it is this Easter with us. Jesus is ever leading us on, out of sorrow and sadness and despair, to a fresh revelation of Himself. We are sad. We tell Him our sorrows. We receive His teaching. We constrain Him to abide. He reveals Himself to us anew. We make known the revelation to others. That is the oft-repeated cycle of our own experience. We constrain Him, by prayer, by obedience, by love. He reveals Himself, it may be, in that Breaking of the Bread which is our Eucharist. Each Eucharistic preparation is just an Easter walk with our Lord along the Emmaus road, leading from darkness to light, from disappointment to hope, from loneliness to the sense of the Divine Companionship. The revelation, which Jesus makes, overflows the life and brings its message of joy to others through us. So the world, with its aching search after happiness, will take knowledge that we have been with Jesus, and are with Him continually in all the manifold experiences of life, ever finding inexhaustible comfort and strength in the companionship of our risen Lord.

This meditation, remarkable in its simplicity, shows us the three aspects of the means of grace in Jesus Christ; that he is truly God (who only can redeem us), that he is truly man (who only can identify with us as we are), that he makes himself available to us when and where we need him most. The brief prayer, based on St. Paul (2 Cor. 13:14) and called simply The Grace, sums it up: "The grace of our Lord Jesus Christ, and the love of God, and the fellowship of the Holy Ghost, be with us all evermore."

The phrase "the love of God" is often misleading. It

seems sometimes to describe a wide, placid, misty ocean of love into which one disappears or upon which one floats and thereby ceases to have problems. Some appear to have found comfort in such a contemplation. But it is not the biblical picture. In that account God deals with people as they are and in real terms. It is true that Moses is arrested in the desert by the appearance of a bush which seems to be on fire but is not burned up and it is true that in the traditional story he hears the "voice" of God. It is also true that God's purpose for Moses and for His people works itself out in the events of history—some of these events quite unpleasant. The root fact is that God involves Himself not in a misty way but in an actual way and in real events. As in the offer of salvation, so the love of God is alive and not static. It is the *lovingness* of God, His good will in action.

An intelligent woman on a college faculty, struggling with acceptance of the Christian faith, once wrote to me, "If one believes, it shouldn't be because how awful if we didn't . . . help, help. It should be because the presence of God is a transcendent reality which gives content and meaning to life. Love *is* the great power. But how many people love anything but themselves? Precious few. That's what revolts me about some religiousites. They talk more about soaking up God's love than in loving God. It is the loving that transforms, not the being loved. . . . God isn't particularly concerned about our security, I fancy. Rather about our risk."

It is the loving that transforms, not the being loved. When one is in love one has two motives. The first is to serve the beloved in any way possible; the second is the desire to become the person the beloved thinks one is (though one knows he is not and has a secret fear of being discovered), and to do so for that other person's sake.

This is equally true of our love of God, with one significant difference. It is true that when one loves God even a little that one wishes to serve Him. "Serve the Lord with gladness and come into his presence with a song." This is worship, the glad response to the love of God, the thanksgiving. It is also true that the dynamic for Christian living is God's view of us, His good will toward us. So we may begin to act like the person God sees in us all the time. Religion always precedes morality, is the reason for it. Faith precedes ethics. Delight in God is the spring of right living.

The significant difference is that God, who knows all about us, loves us unconditionally. The Christian, Charles Williams reminds us, is literally "in love." That is where he is. God is not fooled but neither is He ever less than Himself, pouring out in the person of Christ the expense of love necessary to redeem mankind. This is the means of grace.

It follows from this that one can see Christ in every man, not in the sense of little Christs but in the sense of the broken image in every man whom the Lord comes to redeem. The Russian writer, Turgenev, records this insight from his youth:

I saw myself, a youth, almost a boy, in a low-pitched wooden church. The slim wax candles gleamed, spots of red, before the old pictures of the Saints. There stood before me many people, all fair-haired peasant heads. From time to time they began swaying, falling, rising again, like the ripe ears of wheat when the wind in summer passes over them. All at once a man came up from behind and stood beside me. I did not turn towards him, but I felt that the man was Christ. Emotion, curiosity, awe overmastered me. I made an effort and looked at my neighbor. A face like everyone's, a face like all men's faces.

The eyes looked a little upward, quietly and intently; the lips closed, not compressed; the upper lip as it were resting on the other; a small beard parted in two; the hands folded and still; and the clothes on him like everyone's. "What sort of Christ is this?" I thought. "Such an ordinary, ordinary man. It cannot be." I turned away, but I had hardly turned my eyes from this ordinary man when I felt again that it was really none other than Christ standing beside me. Suddenly my heart sank and I came to myself. Only then I realized that just such a face is the face of Christ—a face like all men's faces.

Jesus was crucified not on a cathedral altar between two candles but on a cross between two thieves, outside the city walls in a place accursed. The crowds stood far off, the only people close at hand those who had to be there: the bored soldiers playing dice to while away the time, the curious centurion who was in command, the mystified and despairing disciples constrained by love. The world passed by, reading the sign in its own languages as the world does. In death as in life the Universal Man is in the middle of the world's hurt, receiving over and over again all that is worst in us and all that is best.

In the face of this the Christian is one who is freed to accept himself (it need not be harder for him than it is for God!), who is able to have meaningful relationships with other people—to accept from them, to enjoy them. And, quite unconsciously, he will show forth on his little stage the love of God in thanksgiving.

If you were to die tonight and be presented at the bar of final appeal, what would you plead in your defense? Would you call to witness your keen intelligence? I doubt it. Would you plead your goodness over the years? I doubt it. Would you invoke your good intentions? I think not. What then *would* you plead as your means of grace and your hope of glory? There would be only one possible chance—that the evil you had done had been absorbed by the only one capable of absorbing it, that your good intentions (however feeble) had been perceived for what they were and judged generously, that your case had been taken and pleaded by the Savior who had died in your place.

It would be the opposite of Peter's thoughtless speech of the world, "Behold, we have forsaken all, and followed thee; what shall we have therefore?" (Matt. 19:27). The answer to Peter's question is, "All that you can accept." For the means of grace and the hope of glory are the same thing.

St. Paul writes to the Colossians, "Christ in you, the hope of glory" (1:27), which is the origin of the phrase in the General Thanksgiving. One modern translation says, "the hope of all the glorious things to come." This glory, we are told in Scripture, is to be with Christ, to enjoy the companionship of the risen and glorified Lord, and to merit his approval. The imagery is that of light, of radiance, which is one of the constant themes of the Bible. There is a direct connection between "Let there be light" (Gen. 1:3) and "I am the light of the world" (Jn. 8:12), between "The people that walked in darkness have seen a great light" (Isa. 9:2) and "That was the true Light, which lighteth every man that cometh into the world" (Jn. 1:9), between "Arise, shine; for thy light is come" (Isa. 60:1) and "Awake thou that sleepest, and arise from the dead, and Christ shall give thee light" (Eph. 5:14).

This is the glorious morning, the day of the Lord, the radiance which is Christ. The good life is not something that we do, but the life of the crucified and risen Lord in us, accepted by faith. It is not a course of action calculated to make us good in the eyes of God—that is impossible—but a life lived out in thanksgiving because God has been, and continues to be, so good to us. The means of grace and the hope of glory are God's offer of Himself in the good companionship of Jesus Christ our Lord.

VIII

. . . And, we beseech thee,
give us that due sense of all
thy mercies, that our hearts may be
unfeignedly thankful . . .

Faith, itself a gift of God, is also the means by which we accept and use His good gifts. This is true not only in regard to the person of Christ our Savior, the greatest gift, but also of countless smaller gifts and relationships. In fact, none of us could get along from day to day in our ordinary concerns and activities without faith. Let me illustrate. Suppose that you have accepted a friend's invitation to dinner for a certain day at a certain hour. You confidently expect to be there and your friend confidently looks forward to your being there. If you have known each other for some time the host might be able to guess with some accuracy that the guest is likely to forget the date or to come late, while the guest might be able to predict that the host will forget that he had invited anyone or that dinner will be late or that it will be served on time. In other words there will be a case history, a probability curve. But if they are to meet at all they must both proceed on an act of faith, which takes up where probability leaves off. Nothing can be proved in advance. After the date both persons can say with historical accuracy that the dinner date did or did not take place as expected or that such and such happened. To put the process in some sort of order, we have: proposal, expectation, probability, event—and each of these is dependent upon faith.

Take another example. Suppose a young man and a young woman come to know each other quite well during their college days. They have had a number of dates and enjoy each other's company. Then one night the young man says, "Mary, I love you with all my heart; will you marry me?" What does Mary do? She adds up all the facts and impressions she has about this boy. She has been doing this, as has he, for some time, but now she has to put the data in order and draw up a sort of balance sheet in the face of the direct question. It may be "so sudden," but it is not very likely. She will strike a trial balance on how he measures up in general, a sort of average of their times together. She will ask herself how this man is regarded by his other friends, how he acts when everything goes wrong, what his long-term interests seem to be. She will wonder about life with him for fifty years or so. She will imagine herself introducing him as her husband to the people she loves and respects most. She may well be influenced by the attitude of her parents toward this boy or by her attitude toward his parents. She will ask herself how she would like this man to be the father of her children. She will probably discuss the proposal, at some length, with a close friend or two.

Having assembled and arranged this rather impressive body of data Mary will find that she has a probability curve, but no more. She has come to a jumping-off place. If she does say, then or later, "Yes, John, I will marry you," she is taking a leap into the unknown future, based on the best she knows. She can prove nothing in advance. Years later she (and he) will be able to say a number of things, but now they must proceed on faith if they are to proceed at all. And there is one more consideration. Only after Mary has agreed to marry John does she begin to wonder if she really wants to! Only after the agreement has been made do the real doubts arise; before this time they were speculations and relatively inexpensive.

All of these elements are present and operable when we are confronted with the proposition of belief in a loving God as He has revealed Himself in Jesus Christ. Men have always sought for proof of the existence of God, forgetting sometimes that God—the biblical God, maker of all things, judge of all men—is infinite while we are finite. God is unlimited, men are limited; we cannot catch God in a noose of our own reasoning. The proofs of God are interesting and indicative but not conclusive. The simplest of them is the familiar argument from design. The universe in which we live is an orderly universe; the planets keep their orbits in their path around the sun, night follows day, and when mutations occur they are seen as deviations from a describable norm. It is argued from this that since order, whenever we observe it, presupposes an orderer—an agent who creates the state of order—then orderliness in the universe demands the existence of a Universal Orderer.

The trouble with this argument, as argument, is that it really proves nothing at all; what it does is to demonstrate a high degree of probability. At the end of it, as at the end of any of the classical proofs, one can say, "It could be." But that is all.

Another type of proof is the argument from collective religious experience. This argument observes that many people in different times and places seem to have found the Christian faith believable and to have believed it; further, that most of the humanitarian aspects of what we loosely call Western Civilization are derived from the Christian faith. The trouble is that the observation, however true, does not necessarily apply to the person doing the observing. It is impersonal.

An old illustration might be helpful here. Let us suppose that you wish to teach a child to swim and that you begin by attempting to get across to him the fact that swimming is possible. You might talk about the buoyancy of water in quantity, about the ability of the human body to float under certain circumstances, about the possibility of a person propelling himself through the water by moving his arms and legs in a particular manner. This will sound—and does!—theoretical and academic, but no more so than the standard proof system to demonstrate the existence of God. Both indicate a degree of probability. At the end of the lecture the child could say, "It could be." But, again, that would be all.

Now suppose that you take this boy out onto the dock and show him another boy swimming. The boy, observing another swimming, could say, "It appears to be possible for *him*." This would be comparable to the second argument, as if to say, "Consider all the people in history, including those you yourself have known, who appear to believe in the Christian faith, the revelation of God in Christ."

Ultimately, the nonswimmer can be convinced of his ability to swim only when he gives his own body to the buoyancy of the water in an act of faith, moves his arms and legs, and discovers that it holds *him* up. Then he can say with conviction beyond argument, "I know it is possible to swim because I swam; I was there, I was doing it."

So it is with our religious faith. We can never find God by way of an intellectual hunting expedition (though such a process may make it possible for us to move closer to the event of believing), nor by way of speculation about the faith of others (though this may encourage us to make the leap of faith ourselves). Like the boy in the story we can know the reality only through personal encounter. But once we have entered into the life of God through accepting His outreach for us in Christ the Lord, the world of ideas and the events of history take on new meaning and importance for us. Tertullian, a second-century convert, said, "I believe in order that I may know."

The Christian faith takes a lot of believing. It is not easy for us, who love ourselves so much and who think of everything in terms of how it affects us, to contemplate a God who knows and loves us completely and all the time and without conditions. A contemporary theologian says, "The existence of God is known by an act of madness, daring and love: it is to throw the thread of life into the heavens in the certainty that it will take hold there without any guarantees of causality; it is a dumb beseeching act, it is a prayer." At first reading this may seem a strange, even a shocking statement, but it is true I am sure that

God cannot be proved, only experienced. Out of this act of faith, this dare, comes our knowledge of God through living with Him.

By now you may be wondering what all of this has to do with the phrase at the head of this chapter. A "due sense" of the mercies of God implies an openness to receive and respond to these mercies. This, in turn, implies acts of faith that God's gifts, especially the gift of Himself are being offered and can be received. This is the texture of the Christian life. And "due sense" implies some knowledge of what the mercies of God mean. Let me illustrate this symbolically and then actually.

There is a passage in St. Mark (8:22-25) which describes how a blind man of Bethsaida was brought to Jesus to be healed. He took him by the hand and led him out of the town. Then he put his hands on his eyes and asked him if he saw anything. The blind man said, "I see men as trees, walking." Jesus put his hands on the man's eyes again "and made him look up: and he was restored, and saw every man clearly."

Often we see men as trees because our eyes are not open, or are out of focus, or because our vision is dimmed. We have not looked up. We have to look again before we see things as they really are. But once we have seen, we know. A much longer account of the healing of a blind man fills the whole ninth chapter of the Gospel according to St. John. There is a larger cast of characters and a lot more conversation but one clear phrase stands out as nonarguable. The man is being questioned closely by a group who wish to make it appear that the event did not take place as described. He finally counters their denials by saying, "One thing I know, that, whereas I was blind, now I see." A fact is a fact.

Sometimes we come to a due sense of God's mercies

because of the slow unfolding of our awareness of a merciful God and of the manner in which He deals with us. Sometimes the revelation comes suddenly, dramatically, in a moment. And from that time on we know, in a certain hard core of conviction, which may be often questioned but never blotted out. This is like the boy who swam and knew he was doing it.

I once had to deal with a couple who had lost their only child, a little girl, almost overnight. She had been attacked by some mysterious virus and though she was rushed to the hospital and had every possible help there never was much hope. In a matter of hours the child was dead. The shock was a severe one for the parents and their emotional climate straight through to the time of burial was one of merciful numbness.

The day of the funeral was a cold, raw November day in New England with rain falling slowly from a steel gray sky. When the little coffin was lowered into the ground I could feel the hearts of that father and mother going down with it. Their faces were blank. For them there was darkness over all the land from the sixth hour unto the ninth hour. Everything was finished.

After the funeral I went back with them to their house. They were poor people—the man worked in the local mill—and had very little to go on. We sat in the kitchen and made some coffee. Nobody had much to say. In fact, on such occasions one feels that he ought either to remain silent or to say as simply as possible the best thing he knows. So I tried. I said I believed that it was impossible for any person to move outside of the circle of God's loving concern. I could not say exactly where their child was but I was sure about God. It was as if the circle of God's love were like the circumference of a wheel; somewhere within it was this man and this woman and their child. They meet, as the spokes do, in the hub of the wheel which is the reality of God and His compassion. This is what makes our prayers for each other real; we speak to each other of God's care for us all.

The other piece of saving truth is that there is a bottom in this desperate sense of loss, and that is Christ Himself. No person in a time of bleak, cold, agonizing loneliness can stand in a place where God in Christ has not already stood. The other end of "Who for us men and for our salvation came down from heaven," is "My God, my God, why hast thou forsaken me?" It was necessary in the plan of redemption for our Lord, in His human nature, to know the sense of the loss of God's presence; not the loss of God's presence, for that is impossible, but the sense of that loss. That is the worst thing there is, and Jesus was there. If these terrible words were to be stricken out of the Gospel no others could take their place. One cannot fall through into nothingness; that is where God is.

So it is that God uses quite ordinary people in a quite ordinary kitchen on a November afternoon to teach each other the healing truth of His loving-kindness. And so it is that a chink of light appears, perhaps, in the darkness; enough to light the way for a step or two. And so it is that the due sense of God's mercy begins to be real. We are grateful not only for the glory of a fresh morning when the world seems to have just washed its face, but for compassion in the midst of tragedy, for companionship in anguish, for the victory of the Cross which becomes our victory in faith.

Let us turn to the second part of our chapter heading, "that our hearts may be unfeignedly thankful." It is possible to be trivially thankful or casually thankful—I am sure that each of us has been so—but this is a pale imitation of real thanksgiving. The trouble is that a little religion can inoculate us against the real thing. A little religion is a nuisance, just enough to make us uncomfortable without giving us freedom. Triviality is one of the deadliest sins, along with artificiality, conformity for its own sake, unwillingness that our eyes should be opened. They are all forms of insulation from God, they are all feigning. They are fakes in the place of reality.

If a wife saves up for months from the housekeeping money to buy her husband an expensive present—something he really wants but does not feel they can afford—and gives it to him, he is likely to have two reactions. Because of their love and his knowledge of what the present must have cost he will probably say, "You shouldn't have done it." What this really means is, "I am not worth it." This is genuine humility, objectivity. But the fact is that he is worth it to her. And that is the spring of the second reaction which is genuine thanksgiving, unfeigned.

Similarly, when we begin to have some idea (we can never have more than a little) of the expense to God of our salvation we can say, and mean, "I am not worth it." But the worthiness is there just the same, bestowed by God's love for us. And the result is a thankful heart and a thankful life.

During World War II a man with a clipped British accent hailed me in South Station, Boston, and asked if I were "Church of England." I said that I was and he introduced his two friends. They turned out to be officers from a British cruiser which had been in some heavy action and was in port for repairs. They had not been ashore since they left Plymouth some months before and were looking for a place to walk. The upshot was that I took them home with me to Gloucester and we walked together on the moors of Cape Ann until we had worked up an appetite for supper. None of them had ever been in the United States before and there were lots of questions. By the time a leisurely supper was over and I had taken them back to Boston we had spent several hours together. Driving home alone I could not help wondering what sort of impression they had of what they had seen and heard: the North Shore of Massachusetts, city and country, my home and family, my answers to their questions. What did they think of me as a Christian, for there I was posing as one?

So with our thanks, I think, feigned or unfeigned. It shows. And it springs from a due sense of God's mercies. Saying "thank you" may mean something or nothing at all. Being thankful means that we know something of our need and something about the way God responds to it. True thanksgiving, for a Christian, goes straight through to the person of Christ. This is our faith and our life on good days and bad, in comedy or tragedy, at Cana or Calvary.

"The Lord is my Light" is theology and good theology; "The Lord is *my* Light" is faith.

IX

. . . and that we show forth thy praise, not only with our lips, but in our lives . . .

We show forth the praise of God and we do it together, if we do it at all, because we live in community. No man can be a church or a community or a family all by himself. He may represent any or all of these bodies but only because he has come out of them. Simeon Stylites, on his pillar, is an object of curiosity more than anything else. Life does not flow through him, it is not shared.

When a child is born he is the product of a group; it would appear a group of two but each of these two persons is a similar group product with the lines widening backward, farther than the mind can reach. When the child is reborn into Christian community in baptism the Church says, "We receive this child into the congregation of Christ's flock."

The world is full of lonely people, people who feel unwanted, unrelated, unloved ("If I should die who would miss me?"). This is no new thing; it is as old as the world. Homer speaks of one who is "unwept, unhonoured and uninterred" (Sir Walter Scott says "unwept, unhonoured and unsung"). The author of the book Ecclesiasticus says, "And some there be, which have no memorial; who are perished, as though they had never been; and are become as though they had never been born" (44:9). In his extremity Job felt that even God had left him. He cries out, "Oh that I knew where I might find him! . . . Behold, I go forward, but he is not there; and backward, but I cannot perceive him: On the left hand, where he doth work, but I cannot behold him: he hideth himself on the right hand, that I cannot see him" (23:3, 8, 9).

On the secular level we are concerned about this, so much so in fact that we have invented a whole new profession whose chief duty is to listen to us, even if we have to hire them to do it. Books about personal counseling and group therapy pour off the presses. Catchwords, like "togetherness" get run into the ground and inspire cartoonists. Yet, at the back of all this one of our basic human needs is being revealed, the need to be "we" in a meaningful way.

The Church is not a collection of people, nor even an organization of people. It is a body of people, united in Christ the Lord. This is a part of what St. Paul means when he calls the Church the "body of Christ." It is an organism in which people find their meaning, as cells in a living body, and whose purpose is the salvation of mankind

because this is the purpose of Christ. It follows from this
that the members of the body have a necessary relationship to one another.

All of the early attempts to describe the Church, this
new creature unlimited by boundaries of race or class or
category, were partial and incomplete. They were efforts
to catch in words the nature of a community which was
as wide and as deep and as practical as the love of God
made known to us in Jesus Christ. Among the early names
were "the colony of heaven," "the worshiping fellowship,"
"the friends of Jesus," "the followers of the way," "the
new life." The thread running through all of these, the
ruling idea, is that of a community which is in the
world but not of it. Its manners are different, its definition
of success is different, its idea of how to have a good time
is different. The Christian is not lonely (though sometimes he chooses to be alone) because he is accepted and
sustained by the brethren who know themselves to be accepted and sustained by God. He can afford not to be
afraid because he knows the good companionship of God
in Christ with whom he walks, even through the valley
of the shadow of death.

Now it is quite true that the local exhibit of the Christian
Church does not always act this way, for reasons to
which we have already given some attention; but this
does not alter what it is. It is interesting that the Church's
own nature is used as a criterion by which to measure its
shortcomings. When church people are criticized for back-
biting or gossip they are really being criticized for acting
inappropriately according to the Church's standards. There
is a difference between the Church's standards and the
world's; there also is all the difference in the world
in resources. When people say that the Church is full of
hypocrites they are, of course, telling the truth. But so is

the world outside of the Church full of hypocrites. Wherever they are, people are souls divided, tensions, little civil wars. This is not news to a Christian. In fact it is one of the reasons why he is a member of the Church; he comes as a divided person in need of wholeness, a sinner in need of salvation. And having come, he finds himself in the company of many like himself on the same pilgrimage. And there he joins in saying, "We show forth thy praise . . . for all thy goodness and loving kindness to us and to all men." The Church is that body of people which is knit together in thanksgiving for God and for one another.

Showing forth praise in the family of God takes many forms. People do not necessarily have to do what we expect them to do in order to be pleasing to God. I recently heard this observation: "A woman should be able to cook for God in the church and send what she cooks to the sick or the old, and not be asked to serve on a committee." I agree, and if the body of praisers is alive this sort of thing will go on. It is also true that there are those who would like to serve on committees and who can make their offering that way to some purpose. They may need a free baby-sitter, though, as another person's offering.

We get confused sometimes about church work. Basically and continually our proper work in the body of Christ is the round of prayer and praise to almighty God. All the other good and necessary things—whether money-raising or cake-baking or committee meetings—are secondary. It is when we lose sight of this central truth that the Church begins to look a lot like the surrounding world and stops redeeming it. Worship *is* the glad response to the love of God. He made the world and it is good. He made us to know Him and to love Him and to enjoy Him forever. In our extremity He took our place and acted for us, blotting out our sin and offering us union with Him again. It is our response to this givenness, and in thanksgiving for our redemption, that we discover the delight of God's created world and our relation to one another in it. So we come together to sing unto the Lord, to lift up our hearts and to give thanks. It is the best thing we can do and in making this act of praise we discover how the arts of tone and color, chiseled line and printed word can sing to the glory of God. After that it is possible to have a community and the reason for the feeding of the poor becomes plain.

Recently I heard quite a wise observation on the part of a girl who has grown just old enough to be included in the conversation of people who drop in to visit her parents. She said, "I have noticed that people are either open or shut." I had a pretty good idea of what she meant but drew her out a bit anyway. She explained thoughtfully that people seemed to come in three categories. There were those who treated her as if she were a piece of furniture or, at best, an animated lazy-susan. And there were those, unable to relate to a child, who made polite noises and fell back on standard clichés as, "My, how you have grown," as if they expected her to shrink and were pleasantly surprised that she had not done so. Thirdly, there was a small group of people who, without effort, treated her as if she were herself, an alive and growing and interested human being. She realized that this took a little imagination and a willingness to put out some conversational planks that led someplace. She had begun to see that listening can be creative.

I think she is right on all counts and I have a theory that the open people are that way because they are open to receive as well as to give. Their aliveness, their ability to respond, springs from a fundamental thanksgiving for life and the gifts of life—ultimately thanksgiving for the goodness of God. William Law, the eighteenth-century religious writer, thinks that this is the essential quality that makes a saint. He says, "Would you know who is the greatest saint in the world? It is not he who prays most or fasts most; it is not he who gives most alms, or is most eminent for temperance, chastity or justice; but it is he who is always thankful to God, who wills everything that God wills, who receives everything as an instance of God's goodness, and has a heart always ready to praise God for it."

An interesting speculation might be what each of us would do if we had but one more day to live and knew it. I once gave this problem to a group of college students, asked them to think about it for fifteen minutes or so, without discussion, then write their answers without signing their names. The answers were various but they had one element in common and one singular omission. The variety included letters home (to say good-by) and to a number of people (to say various things). Some mentioned paying back borrowed money, some wanted to admit cheating on an examination paper, some planned apologies to persons wronged in the past. Several wanted to see a particular person for the last time, several said they would spend the day in prayer and meditation, others said they would confess their sins to God. And so it went.

You will have noticed the element in common, that each of them on the last day planned to do things that ought to be done anyway; they had simply not found time for it somehow. And not a single one mentioned being thankful for the gifts of the past and present, though this may have been implied. But these people were young and "rich beyond avarice in the golden spoils of time." When one is young death is something that happens to other people, there is plenty of time. Looking through the other end of the telescope Walter de la Mare says, "Look your last on all things lovely, every hour."

What would you or I do in such a day? What would be uppermost in our minds? Certainly some of the considerations already mentioned might well have a place, but would fear win out over thanksgiving? I wonder. A mature Christian, a safe (saved) and thankful (converted) person, would probably do very little differently if he knew this to be his last day. But the words of the general Thanksgiving might ring in his ears. The substance of it is in the words of a godly old man, Simeon, when he beheld the Christ-child, 'Lord, now lettest thou thy servant depart in peace, according to thy word. For mine eyes have seen thy salvation" (Lk. 2:29, 30).

The second phrase of our chapter heading, "not only with our lips, but in our lives," is both a self-accusation and a hope. Surely for all of us there is a large gap between what we profess and what we do, between promise and performance. We all talk a better game than we play, we all want to be liked. So we talk about it. We say things to be pleasing or acceptable. This is especially true with chance met acquaintances. The person fate gives us as a seatmate on a train or plane is apt to be the giver and receiver of astonishing confidences—after all, we will probably never see each other again—but the underlying feeling tone is one of agreement. When we stand up at the end of the journey and say, "It has been pleasant to share your company, we are also saying, "I hope you liked me, too." There is nothing wrong in this but it is inexpensive. There is nothing to be questioned or tested by time or lived out. It is a parenthesis in one's life. I know a person who adopts a different role every time he takes a trip, invents a new life for himself and supports it with a great deal of circumstantial detail. He says he enjoys this fantasy, it relaxes him, and I am sure he makes a considerable impression. I doubt there is much harm in this either, as long as the man really knows where reality stops and fantasy begins (no mean trick in itself!) and is doing it for entertainment. But I am sure that the people back home would be amazed at the recounting of his exploits.

It is much harder to live out our lives, day by day and year by year, among those who know us as we know them. There is an old story about Mark Twain's * involvement with a Bible-reading family in his courting days. The family would gather in the evening before bedtime to listen while Father read a chapter. The story goes that Mark, offered the privilege of reading one night, made up a narrative in biblical language, supposedly from the book of Genesis, which his future father-in-law spent a good deal of time trying to find! But the made-up story is interesting in itself. A traveler, it seems, appeared at the door of the tent of the patriarch Abraham asking for food and lodging. He was invited in and made welcome. The meal was about to be served when Abraham noticed that his guest had not purified himself in the proper manner and, forthwith, kicked him out supperless. That night God appeared to the patriarch in a dream and said, "Abraham, I have put up with that man all his life. I think you might have stood him for a night!"

I suppose that for all of us, the closer the bond between lips and lives, the closer we are to being whole people. In this prayer we ask God's help that this may be so. The self-accusation is that it is not so, the hope that it may be. But there is a helpfulness in the self-accusation when it is done in honesty. In the Gospel there

* This story has also been attributed to Benjamin Franklin.

is a gallery of people who judge themselves in the presence of Jesus, who is the Truth in person: Peter in the fishing boat, Mary Magdalene, the rich young man, the soldier whose son was sick, Pontius Pilate, the thief dying on a cross. And always, ourselves.

Facing reality, including the truth about oneself, is always both difficult and defining—there it is—but it may be the first step toward a change for the better. The life of our Lord is the only place where we see lips and life completely at one but it is this very fact, coupled with our faith that it was for our salvation that God became man, which gives us hope. In his perfect manhood we are given an example of a whole man; in the work of Christ we are given the means of becoming whole. Judgment (telling the truth) and grace (love in action) are offered at the same time by the same person.

One of the insights into any person's character is the way in which he deals with helpless minorities—social, racial, political, economic—people from whom he can derive no advantage. In a more elegant age it used to be said that no one knows the great man better than the great man's valet. We show ourselves to our children and to those who work with us and to those who do us service. It comes down to how much we are willing to give away for nothing. And the thought behind that is how aware we are of what we have been given for nothing—"Who for us men and for our salvation. . . ." In the end gentleness is the strongest thing, compassion is the door into life.

A phrase we sometimes use, "to make peace," is quite literal. We make peace or fail to do so every day, not in some dreadful "do-gooder" or "thought-control" way, but in ourselves, in our attitude to those we meet, especially those from whom we can derive no advantage. I rather think that when statesmen gather to make a treaty of peace that they cannot invoke more peace—more will to peace—than there *is,* and that such peace as there is comes from countless small encounters.

Each person, each combination of lips and life, has a sphere of influence mostly, I think, unknown to that person. Our largest influence is an unconscious one. Furthermore, our opportunities for influence are frequently so close at hand as to go unnoticed. A story about Bishop Phillips Brooks comes to mind. The bishop had preached a sermon about the missionary outreach of the Church— the world community, the imperative on Christians to speak about what they have received. After the sermon a quite ordinary man came to him and said that he was moved by the bishop's words but that his own life lay in a small compass with no journeyings to heathen lands, that he saw little relevance in the sermon for people like himself. The bishop heard him out, then asked him what he did for a living. The man replied that he was a railroad engineer.

"Is the fireman a Christian?"

"I don't know."

"Well, you might start there!"

The Church has had quite a lot to say about lips. Jeremiah says, "Their tongue is as an arrow shot out." St. James says, "The tongue is a fire . . . The tongue can no man tame." But St. Paul speaks about building up the body of Christ by that which every person in his own way supplies, about "speaking the truth in love." We need to know the truth but, just as much, we need the healingness of love when it is spoken. Words can wound and maim and kill. Words also can heal and restore. Every one of us has said things which he wishes (sometimes desperately) that he had not said, but the words have be-

come a part of the permanent record. They can sometimes be taken back but they cannot be unsaid. And
each of us has said things (probably now forgotten) for
which another person has been grateful, restored, quick-
ened.

As children of God our chief duty and joy is to praise
Him who made us, redeemed us and sustains us on our
way. This is our thanksgiving. And in living it out, lips
and lives may begin to become one.

*. . . by giving up our selves to thy
service, and by walking before thee
in holiness and righteousness
all our days . . .*

We sometimes hear it said that a Christian should be selfless. Nothing, of course, could be farther from the truth. There is nothing ghostly about the Christian religion; its nature requires a body through which a will is expressed, just as God's saving good will is expressed bodily in Jesus Christ our Lord. In fact Christian doctrine about personality envisions not its absence but, rather, its fullest expression. The Epistle to the Ephesians says, "Till we all come in the unity of the faith, and of the knowledge of the Son of God, unto a perfect man, unto the measure of the stature of the fulness of Christ." (4:13) It is in beginning to know and to accept our real selves (because God does) that we have something to give away to the service of God.

Most of us have known the experience of being at our best in the company of some special person. Not a censorious person from whom we try to conceal our true nature but a loving and understanding person who makes us blossom, in whose company our best self seems like our real self. Such a person is a blessing, a redeemer. Some schoolteachers have this quality, the ability to see in a boy or girl not only what appears on the outside but the essential person inside waiting to be discovered. This mysterious and creative encounter is one of the aspects of thankful living. Such a person sees and hears and waits but, most of all, he is glad to be alive in God's world. So he is able to see what there is to be seen.

I have suggested that people judge themselves in Jesus' presence because he is the Truth. By the same light he discovers people's true selves to themselves. Remember Matthew the publican? Here was a sharp-eyed, nimble-witted tax collector, despised both by his own countrymen and by the foreign government which he served. No one had a good word for Matthew the publican, no one but Christ the Lord who saw him as he really wanted to be and chose him for an apostle. So it is with Zaccheus, Mary Magdalene, Philip and Nathanial and ourselves. Our service to God is our worship, our thanksgiving for His seeing us, trusting us, loving us in the midst of our blighted hopes and broken promises, for acting as if we were worth saving. And our thanks goes out to those in the company of God's faithful people who have eyes to see and hearts to understand.

Our service to God is our freedom because His will is better for us than our own. There is room to move in it, there is no deception, and there is liberty to choose wisely, which is what freedom is.

Just as religion precedes morality, so holiness precedes righteousness. The quest for holiness is the quest of mankind when all other roads to self-understanding have been tried. A few chapters ago we thought about the choices a man faces in answering the question, "What is the purpose of my life?" At the end of it I suggested that the creative answer is in living gladly as children of God, the persons we really are. That is, we find our safety in His love, our freedom in His will for us, our wholeness in His holiness. In God, holiness and righteousness are the same thing for God is one. With us holiness precedes righteousness, if righteousness is to occur at all, because holiness is our likeness to God.

There is an incident in Marc Connelly's delightful and perceptive folk play, *The Green Pastures,* where God is discussing the right person to lead the children of Israel out of Egypt. In the play God is disappointed that more good did not come out of His experiment with the Flood and He consults Isaac about the best man for the new plan.

Isaac: "Does you want de brainiest or de holiest, Lawd?"
God: "I want de holiest. I'll make him brainy."

Holiness, God's quality, is usually unexpected in our lives because we like to think of ourselves as independent or successful or at least adequate. Holiness shows us up to be none of these and at the same time gives us hope. When Jacob says, "Surely the Lord is in this place; and I knew it not," he is being both surprised and expectant. Up to this time he had seemed to himself to be doing very well. Now he is both accused and blessed. But the Lord was

there all the time. T. S. Eliot echoes the experience of
Jacob when he writes:

> *We shall not cease from exploration*
> *And the end of all our exploring*
> *Will be to arrive where we started*
> *And know the place for the first time.*

Moses is surprised when God makes Himself known
to him in the desert saying, ". . . put off thy shoes from off
thy feet, for the place whereon thou standest is holy
ground." It always is. "The world is charged with the
grandeur of God." We draw a line between sacred and
secular which God does not draw. In our secular view we
shut heaven out but God reveals Himself to us in our
commonplaces, illuminating the ordinary with meaning.

The Christian community is nourished by prayer, sacrament and sustaining conversation. In prayer we enter
into communion with the Holy One—adoring, confess-
ing, asking good things for ourselves and our friends,
giving thanks. In the sacraments we know God's invasion
of our lives with adoption, strength and refreshment—
"the outward and visible sign of an inward and spiritual
grace." In sustaining conversation we give and receive our
knowledge of the Mercy, our perception however dim and
inconsistent, that God knits up our brokenness with His
wholeness.

Self-righteousness is the bestowal of a gift on oneself, a
self-reward, without authority to do so or reality in so
doing. The proud Pharisee in our Lord's parable (Lk.
18:9–14) is not telling lies about his virtues or his religious observances; he *did* all those things. His self-righteousness lay in his assurance that he had achieved goodness by
this route. He had given himself a present.

Righteousness consists in being *made* righteous, given a gift, by the one person able to do so, Jesus Christ our Lord. He it is who takes our sins as if they were his own that we may be righteous—justified, forgiven—before God. This is a real transaction, rooted in the stuff of history. The Cross of Christ metaphorically reaches to heaven, poetically it balances that other tree which grew in the midst of the garden. But actually it is planted in the un-poetic soil of a city dump where the best and the worst of mankind meet face to face.

In the Good Friday scene I should like to look at three people in whom we may find reflections of ourselves. They are the dying thief, the centurion, and Barabbas.

The crucifixion of Jesus had one direct and immediate result, the conversion of the thief who spoke to him from his cross. Tradition has named this man Dismas and at least one of our state prisons has a chapel dedicated to him. He represented a sizable group in his place and times, a subject country in a time of political and eco-nomic unrest, shaken by war and the threat of war. He followed a leader, took his chances and got caught. The penalty was severe and savage, death by crucifixion. Now he is at the end of the road. At first Dismas joins his fellow thief in reviling the sufferer between them. In a sense he has to, it is the only way that he can identify with the crowd and relieve his own feelings. But as time wears on under the broiling sun he falls silent and begins to think. He has always wanted to follow a leader who was strong and resourceful. Here is a man who has been called a king. A king? He has dignity, certainly, and courage. He has cursed nobody. Indeed the only words he has said so far are, "Father, forgive them; for they know not what they do"—a sort of royal pardon. Finally he says to his former companion, "Dost not thou fear God, seeing thou art in the same condemnation? And we indeed justly; for we receive the due reward of our deeds: but this man hath done nothing amiss." Then, whether out of reverence or half-mockery or some dimly-realized perception, he turns to Jesus and says, "Lord, remember me when thou comest into thy kingdom." The response is immediate. "And Jesus said unto him, Verily I say unto thee, Today shalt thou be with me in paradise."

There is an unexpected fineness in the penitent thief. He did not bargain, he did not make excuses, he did not explain his hard lot. He simply said, "Lord." The fact that staggered him was not his own sin—that was plain enough—but our Lord's sinlessness. In that moment he saw him, I believe, as he was and judged himself in the presence of the Judge.

There is a sublime simplicity in this scene, as if for an instant the whole drama of salvation were narrowed down to two persons, a dying criminal and the Lord of life. Jesus brought out a quality worth forgiveness in this man which the thief would not have recognized in himself. This is the mercy which makes righteous the unworthy.

The centurion is a professional soldier in a regular army doing a job to which he has been assigned. He knows about authority, he knows about order and he knows about human suffering. He has seen crucifixions before. Instinctively we like this man. He represents the military virtues which are the same in any age, no matter what one thinks about war. He respects good management as well as courage and he has known comradeship in danger and after danger. The army is his way of life.

He has heard of this provincial hero (there have been others) and is mildly interested. He has heard of the entrance into Jerusalem, the palm branches and the mob scene (those excitable Jews!) and he has heard of the riot in the Temple. He has also heard that the authorities are determined to suppress this man. News of the arrest at Gethsemane gets to the barracks, also reports of several trials, the goings and comings, scraps of what this one and that one said. It is no concern of his—a religious squabble with political overtones—until he learns there is to be a crucifixion after all and that he and his men are to carry it out as expeditiously as possible. This country prophet and two thieves are to be crucified outside the Northwest Gate. The time is late morning on Friday.

During the grueling hours of the crucifixion the officer in charge watches and listens. He hears the unusual, almost incredible, words of pardon—"Father, forgive them. . . ." He listens when the robber speaks. A king? He observes the tiny group of disciples at the foot of the cross, whose love has made them bold. But mostly he sees the best he knows lived out and transcended into a new dimension of meaning. At the end of it, when it is finished, he exclaims, "Truly this man was the Son of God" (Mk. 15:39). St. Luke has, "Certainly this was a righteous man."

The centurion represents the decent, practical, uncommitted man of the world. He is decent because he is a member of a society which he respects. He is practical because he lives in a real world. He is personally uncommitted to a religious practice because, so far, he has seen no one to whom he could give his wholehearted commitment. He is ready enough to commit himself to the strong Son of God—if he knew him. This man is not self-righteous; he has been made righteous but this he does not know. There are many of him. Often he is put off from finding the Christ by sentimentalism, by halfhearted Christians, by lovelessness (the righteous elder brother), by the fact that we ourselves perhaps have not met the

Lord—"the means of grace and the hope of glory."

Barabbas, the acquitted, is Everyman. He is the person whose place was taken on that first Good Friday as our place is taken by the Person willing and able to do so, that our new life may begin.

It was a custom every year at Passover time for a prisoner to be released by popular demand. The crowd described in the Gospels, stirred up to clamor for the release of Barabbas, was milling about in the large, square, stone pavement called Gabbatha—the approach to Pilate's hall of judgment. The shouts of the people could easily be heard by Barabbas as he waited under sentence of death in his prison on the Via Dolorosa. Here his life hung in the balance while Jesus, the other prisoner, went from the Sanhedrin (the Jewish religious court) to Pilate, to Herod and back to Pilate.

We are not concerned here with the order of the trial but with the meaning of the man Barabbas. In the case of Dismas we see the whole drama of redemption momentarily narrowed down to two persons; in this case the whole of mankind is represented, in its need and in its blindness, by this brigand under sentence of death. It is God Himself who takes his place, God who in His saving action sets him free.

A man condemned to death has time to think. After he has gone over the immediate situation, hour after hour, he begins to think back about the way he has traveled. He may begin to get a little perspective. No man is born a criminal. He may not have had much to go on but there were probably some who had hopes for him, and he did make choices. After a while the choices shaped into a pattern, eventually into a way of life. He knows what the penalty might be if he got caught but he does not think about it much. Then it happens. He is caught.

The legal wheels grind, he finds himself condemned and he has time on his hands. But not enough. Each day brings the end nearer. He wishes that tomorrow were a larger place. He wonders, if he had his life to live over again, if he would make the same choices. Maybe. He does not know. But he wishes that he had the chance to find out.

This, then, is Barabbas—Everyman—in his prison. He hears the shouts and wonders what is really going on. Presently the shouting dies down and the prisoner's hopes with it. There is a pause, after which the jailer opens the door and says, "Well, Barabbas, you lucky devil, you're a free man!"

"What do you mean?"

"I mean the crowd kept yelling for you till Pilate washed his hands of the whole affair—actually washed them right there—and the prophet fellow is going to be crucified. He's taking your place. What a break!"

Slowly, wonderingly, Barabbas stumbles out of prison, blinking his eyes in the strong sunlight. He is free. He has a tomorrow. He has a whole new life! And it is a gift. It is so that we are made righteous, freed, raised from the dead, given new life—unearned and undeserved. This is the heart of St. Paul's message. He writes, "While we were yet helpless, at the right time Christ died for the ungodly. Why, one will hardly die for a righteous man—though perhaps for a good man one will dare even to die. But God shows his love for us in that while we were yet sinners Christ died for us." (Rom, 5:6–8). And in another place, "You are not your own; you were bought with a price." (1 Cor. 6:19–20).

"All our days" is a long time because it means day after day. All of us are capable of momentary acts of courage, even of heroism, as long as the demand is not sustained for too long a time. We even dramatize ourselves in our moments of valor, especially if there is an audience. The hard thing is bearing pain patiently, facing adversity steadily, enduring humdrum cheerfully, especially without an audience. This is one of the qualities of being grown-up. Life has a certain number of lovely, jewel-like moments; it also has long stretches of monotony. When we pray that we may walk before God in holiness and righteousness all our days, we are asking for a lot. But we are not asking for the impossible because we are talking about the Good Companionship. Christ the Lord has walked this way before and he invites us to join him.

One of our troubles is worry, which is the opposite of faith. We say that we have so many things to do we do not know where to start, so many "oughts" we do not know which one to tackle first, or that we do not know which way to turn. And so we "lose the name of action." Sometimes we tell ourselves these things by way of excuse, or to put off as long as possible the moment when we have to choose *something*—or become vegetables. Sanity lies in picking up a responsibility, doing it as well as we can, and passing on to the next one.

Once when I was a child I made an observation that illustrates this truth, without realizing at the time the meaning of it. I was visiting a farm and had wandered off by myself. After a while I came to a place where I could overlook a railroad and there was a long freight train taking on water before starting up a two-mile grade. I watched the process, interested, and heard the engine puff heavily as it started uphill. Then I heard (I remembered it years later) the sharp click of the couplings as the locomotive picked up one car at a time for the long upgrade. The meaning, of course, was that if the train had been rigid it never could have moved at all. Its progress was made possible by the fact that the loaded cars were picked up one at a time.

God does not ask us to do the impossible. "All our days" would be an impossible assignment if it were one large lump. The fact is that we are on a journey, in the good company of the Risen Christ and in the good company of the saints and sinners he came to set free for the journey. Our response is our faith, our faith is our thanksgiving.

One other perspective: we are tempted to think of our times or our situation as unique, forgetting that we are part of a universal pilgrimage. Outwardly things change daily, the basic human situation remains constant. Gilbert Murray, as quoted by Arthur Darby Nock, says this:

The joy of an Egyptian child of the First Dynasty in a clay doll was every bit as keen as the joy of a child now in a number of vastly better dolls. Her grief was as great when it was taken away. Those are very simple emotions, but I believe the same holds good of emotions much more complex. The joy and grief of the artist is his art, of the strong man in his fighting, of the seeker after knowledge or righteousness in his many wanderings; these and things like them, all the great terrors and desires and beauties, belong somewhere in the permanent stuff of which daily life consists; they go with hunger and thirst and love and the facing of death.

The Christian knows that the stuff of daily life is inhabited by a loving God, and for this he gives thanks.

XI

. . . through Jesus Christ our Lord, to whom, with thee and the Holy Ghost, be all honour and glory, world without end. Amen.

Archbishop William Temple once remarked that the heart of the Christian faith is neither being good nor doing good—these are by-products—but the heart of it is our knowledge and love of a Person, because of whom we can be and do what we could not by ourselves. This is a one-sentence expansion of "through Jesus Christ our Lord."

The word "through" is the key to our understanding of the familiar phrase. We address our prayers and thanksgivings to God in this way not because of our Lord's good example but because of who He is and what He did, the work of Christ. He lived our life and He died our death. He became sin for our sakes that we might be justified (forgiven) in the sight of God. On the cross He took our place, making is possible for us to enter with Him into eternal life.

We cannot live without wanting to be loved, nor without hurting those we love most. The Gospel story of our salvation tells us that at the heart of life God's creating and sustaining and healing love is acted out in spite of everything. It is the opposite of the world's indifference.

My friend, Dean Sherman E. Johnson, writes:

When you see Christ betrayed, and arrested and taken, you are seeing what life is and without illusions. The world is still like that. It too often grinds the innocent under its thoughtless wheels. The Christian is a man or woman who has lost his illusions. But in place of them he has seen a vision. He sees Jesus Christ marching on, to the governor's court and beyond that to Calvary. And he is with Christ, and Christ is with him. This straight, clean young man, still in his early thirties, his life's work apparently wrecked and at an end, is still working, praying, setting men straight, awakening those who are idle and empty and asleep and reconciling his enemies. His love captures even some of those who thought to do him wrong.

Thanksgiving is the answer to fear and an entrance into life. The giving of thanks is the most responsible thing we ever do, the most responsive, the most creative. It is our reply to God the Giver.

Thanks be to God.

Notes

Page

35   Robert Louis Stevenson, *Travels with a Donkey* (London and Toronto: Musson, 1911), p. 105.

38   Christopher Marlowe, *The Tragical History of Dr. Faustus* (1604), edited by F. S. Boas (London: Methuen, 1932), p. 175.

48   Francis Thompson, "The Hound of Heaven," from *Selected Poems* (New York: Scribner, 1930), p. 49.

57   John Donne, *The Sermons*, edited by Evelyn M. Simpson and George R. Potter (Berkeley: University of California Press, 1953), Vol. VI, pp. 153–54. (From a sermon preached at St. Paul's on June 13, 1624, before the Earl of Exeter and his company.)

58   Constance Carrier, "Lisa," from *The Middle Voice* (Denver: Alan Swallow, 1955). Used by permission of the publisher.

60   G. K. Chesterton, *Manalive* (New York: John Lane, 1932).

63   Robert Louis Stevenson, *A Child's Garden of Verses* (London: Longmans, 1885), p. 17.

81–84   F. W. Drake, *The Wondrous Passion* (London: Longmans, 1912), pp. 170–74.

87   Ivan Sergeevich Turgenev, *The Novels and Stories*, trans. Isabel F. Hapgood (New York: Scribner, 1903), section entitled "Poems in Prose," Vol. 16, pp. 365–66.

94 E. Lampert, *The Divine Realm* (London: Faber & Faber, 1943), p. 43.

105 William Law, *A Serious Call to a Devout and Holy Life* (London: W. Innys and J. Richardson, 1753), Vol. 3, p. 278.

113 Marc Connelly, *The Green Pastures* (New York: Rinehart, 1929), p. 109. Used by permission of the publisher.

114 T. S. Eliot, "Little Gidding," from *Four Quartets* (New York: Harcourt, Brace, 1943), p. 39. Used by permission of the publisher.

121 Gilbert Murray, as quoted by Arthur Darby Nock in "Treasure Chest," edited by J. Donald Adams, in *The New York Times.*

123 Sherman E. Johnson, *The Passion according to St. Mark* (pamphlet), preached at St. Mark's, Berkeley, Calif., Good Friday, 1957. Copyright S.E.J. Used by permission of the author.

DATE DUE

'89		